STRETCH MARKS

A MEMOIR

Dear Neil,

The beginning of our story —

LIZ RAPTIS PICCO

L/M Press
391 Old Up Yonder
Santa Cruz, CA 95065

Designed by CreateSpace
Text set in Garamond

Library of Congress Cataloging-in-Publication Data

ISBN-13: 9780615715933 (Pbk)
ISBN-10: 0615715931 (Pbk)

To my mother, Armida Alicia Raptis

and

my mother-in-law, Constance Speers Picco

ACKNOWLEDGEMENTS

There aren't enough words to thank my man, Marty Picco, who always has my back as I write.

I am indebted to Connie S. Picco, Helen Granger, Steve Picco, and Peter M. Raptis Jr. for braving the first draft. Special kudos to The Abbey writing group: Mary Howe, Ellen Reilly, and Eanlai Cronin who challenged me to slow down and dig deeper. I am grateful to Julia Reynolds and Claudia Asbaje Meléndez, *las madrinas,* who came to the rescue with encouragement and margaritas. I am thankful for my dear friends Evelyn Aron, Amy Contardi, Stephanie Gelman, Sierra Knight, and Ana Matiella for listening and plying me with their love.

I thank my lucky stars for Lindsey Alexander, editor extraordinaire who believed in my story, my voice, and kept me on course during the last rounds of revisions. Special thanks to Eanlai Cronin, the best writing partner ever, for bolstering me through innumerable rough patches.

I have a special place in my heart for La Procuraduría de la Defensa del Menor in Ciudad Juárez, Chihuahua, México where my sons were well cared for and loved. I will never forget the fine people of Ciudad Juárez who went over and beyond to help us, especially María, a tenacious lawyer in Mexico City who shepherded our petition. ¡Mil gracias!

This book would not have been possible without my sons, Agustín and Ricardo, who continue to be the sun and the moon in our lives.

TABLE OF CONTENTS

Stretch Marks

PROLOGUE
AUGUST 1998

"Don't lose hope. You'll be home soon," Marty said.

The pay phone signaled with a long nasal beep. My Ladatel card was about to expire. I punched a fresh one-hundred-peso card through the slot, maintaining the only connection I had with my man, my lifeline, who was in northern California while I was trapped in an explosively violent city on the other side of El Paso, Texas. I'd left the comforts of home and embarked on a mission to finalize the adoption of our two toddler sons. Brothers: a bossy but charming four-year-old with sparkling almond eyes, and the ugliest baby I'd ever laid eyes on, whose smile could illuminate a black hole.

"When?" I paced the length of the phone cord, like a dog in its run. Day forty-nine and counting, crossing off each day on the calendar with a black Sharpie until the paper bled. In August the shade became a sauna and the sun a menacing broiler over Ciudad Juárez.

"Tell me. When?" I jerked my hand back from the hot metal fence around the empty pool, a chlorinated stew. The metal railing didn't leave a welt, but etched a crack in my armor.

"I'm sorry," Marty said. I imagined him, feet propped next to his mouse pad, a foggy breeze wafting through his office window, and the promise of a café latte in civilization. I envied him. I wanted to trade places. I wanted to sleep without waking to the boys' cries off and on, all night, the sheets sticky and suffocating. Every night I'd give them sips of cool water, rock the baby in my arms, listen to my oldest longing to go back to the orphanage, and read them a story until they fell asleep. As they slept, I thrashed, while the city seemed to tear itself apart. Sirens wailed non-stop and triggered dogs to howl from one end of the neighborhood to the other. Cars backfired, or were they gunshots? Loud footsteps preceded angry voices and seemed to approach our hollow front door. Would I be able to protect our sons?

"I'm tired of being afraid. I'm tired of barricading the front door with furniture."

"It'll be over soon."

"Soon? The social worker says Family Court made a mistake. A mistake in Santa Cruz means a few extra hours, maybe another day or two, but in Juárez—"

"Don't lose hope, Liz."

"I have at least another six weeks in this hellhole and you don't want me to lose hope. Well, I have news for you, Mr. Picco, there is no hope in Juárez," I spat into the receiver.

My body contracted. I sobbed then sputtered, and stopped when I felt a pair of sticky hands climbing up my legs. I looked down to find Agustín, my four-year-old, crying, clutching his hands, his eyebrows knit together while Ricardo sucked on my left knee. I gathered them close to me, attempting a smile while I rummaged through my backpack and found a linty mint and a sheet of panda stickers that got their attention.

"I'll move my schedule around. I'll be there on Thursday. That's only five more days. You need to call my mom."

"I need to get the hell out of here." I hung up feeling limp and helpless. Getting a phone in our Juárez apartment was out of the question. We weren't Mexican citizens, and our good American credit didn't matter here. By now, my fingerprints were practically embedded on the only pay phone in the courtyard of the apartment complex.

I was grateful the boys didn't understand English. I blew my nose, peeled an orange, and hummed a lullaby while I watched them suck on each section of the fruit until the juice burst from their mouths. I promised them a walk to the park, where a statue of Benito Juárez stood under a canopy of brittle trees, presiding over two ancient goldfish in a murky pond. Our oasis.

I prepared for one more call by setting out a pair of wooden trucks and a rubber ball under the one parched mesquite a few feet away from the pay phone. As the boys played, I looked over my notes, gulping back tears, while the stark reality of the situation taunted me. We would be here for another season. A suffocating darkness entombed my panic. I dialed my mother-in-law's number. My chin quivered, tears blurred my list of next steps, and I wondered what Oprah's experts would say. I was watching the summer reruns for the first time—my escape while the boys napped.

As I waited for the familiar international dial tone, a fierce yank jolted my body. I dropped the receiver. My hair was snatched backward until my eyes locked with the freshly painted courtyard ceiling. I contorted and winced, but couldn't scream. Grabbing for the back of my head, I spun around, ready to fight back, when I smacked into a pair of Dolly Parton boobs spilling out of a gold lamé bathrobe. The shellacked face scowled from above, eyes hidden behind huge gold-framed sunglasses and garnished with brassy orange tousled hair. The Baja Barbie look-alike gripped mortified Agustín by the scruff of the neck. I snatched him from her, shielding the boys behind my rigid body.

"Motherfucking kid won't let me sleep!" She pointed to her window, where my oldest had been bouncing a ball and woke her. She threatened me with a set of six-inch manicured daggers and punctuated each sentence with fuck, bitch, or both. In an instant, I was back behind the junior high gym where "Germ," who sported a Kewpie doll face and calluses on her knuckles, threatened to beat the hell out of me. The familiar girls' gym locker-room mix of eau de cologne and body odor tripped my alarm. I waited for the slap on the face. Instead the woman pivoted, military style, muttering under her breath some people had to work for a living. Her stiletto-heeled sandals clicked on the tiled walkway. Her robe undulated and trailed behind her ala Darth Vader.

How would I do this for another six weeks? I wanted to throw a temper tantrum, but no one would care.

No one I knew would willingly spend a day, much less a summer, in violent, crime-ridden Ciudad Juárez. Of course, back then I believed that I was intelligent, savvy, and organized enough to tackle five different bureaucracies in two countries in less than eight weeks. But I was insane. I mean infertile.

CHAPTER I

DECEMBER 1991

"I'm still pregnant?"

"Yes."

"Impossible." I said, dressed to the nines in sapphire blue from head to toe, waiting in the anemic emergency room of a large Tucson hospital at one in the morning. The nurse continued adjusting the IV needle and didn't bother to reply.

"I just had surgery for an ectopic pregnancy!" I wasn't addressing anyone in particular.

I locked eyes with my husband, who understood my shock at being back in a hospital. He pulled one hand out of his tuxedo pants pocket and raked his floppy hair. A sign of high anxiety. Marty covered me in his arms and stroked my hair in a dreadful silence that blocked out the hallway noise right outside the room. I wanted to break free and run back in time, erase all of this bad luck. Couldn't I just start over?

We had flown in from Santa Cruz, California, two days after Christmas for my older brother's wedding. I had been recuperating from the surgery, but I wasn't going to miss his wedding.

A couple of hours ago, I had been channeling Gloria Estefan at the head of the salsa line, snaking through a glittery hotel ballroom, when I doubled over in a nauseating, overwhelming, dizzying pain. Marty and my younger sister Jannette guided me into a bathroom stall. My husband waited outside in the lobby.

"I shouldn't have danced so much." I stared at my blood-soaked underwear and pantyhose. The blood wasn't coming from the incision above my pubic bone. The terror needled every nerve cell. "Go get Marty."

I watched her close the stall door as I stuffed toilet paper in my underwear and tried to steady myself against the cold metal. I was lightheaded and slipping away when Marty's pinched face snatched me back. He wrapped me up in his coat, my sister gathered my belongings, and the three of us drove to my brother's house a few miles away to call my doctor and change my clothes.

Once in my brother's guest room, I heard the controlled but panicked tone in Marty's voice as he spoke to the on-call Ob/Gyn. He hung up and gently stuffed a towel between my legs, wrapped me up in the bedspread, carried me out to the car, and careened out of the driveway with Jannette in the back seat holding onto me. I felt a thick wetness in between my thighs. Was I hemorrhaging? My mother had almost hemorrhaged to death twice while delivering my younger brothers.

I turned to Marty, whose face was set, but tears were hanging onto the tips of his bottom eyelids. Was I going to die? The hospital lights came into view. Before the car had come to a full stop, Marty blasted the car horn while my sister leapt, yelling at the top of her lungs for help. She is a petite woman only in size.

Later, when my husband recounted the entire episode, I learned my sister stayed with me while he ran to the Triage station and thrust his body over the counter demanding the nurse's attention.

"My wife is hemorrhaging. Her doctor told me to get her here immediately and NOT TO LET YOU MAKE ME WAIT." When Marty turned around, he faced the stunned parents of a young boy who had a compound fractured arm. He apologized and explained that I could die. An emergency team swept me up into a stretcher.

After an eternity, a young doctor with bloodshot eyes and Mozart hair appeared at the doorway announcing his intentions to operate. Again.

I reared up, feeling the tug of the IV in my wrist. "No, with all due respect, you don't understand. My last incision hasn't even healed."

"You have no choice," Dr. S leaned into me and said. "There's over a liter of blood in your belly, I need your consent now."

I signed the forms and, before the news sunk in, a nurse appeared to put a catheter into my urethra. I clamped my legs and shook my head. I looked around for something to hit her with, but everything was either screwed down or too far away.

She took a step back, "I don't blame you honey, but the sooner I do my job, the sooner we can put this behind you. If you feel anything, you can hit me with this." She placed a stethoscope next to my hand. Then she gently spread my legs while she listened to my sister boast about my brother's wedding in great detail. Jannette even took off her coat to model her strapless satin taffeta dress.

When I growled at her for taking too long, the nurse patted my leg, said she was done, and wished me luck. Before my sister left, she hugged me, gave me a blessing, and asked me to pray. I did. The fact remained that a ruptured fallopian tube severed my chances of conceiving.

My grief compounded after the second surgery, even though I feigned hopeful, good spirits during our Easter visit in Arizona. Family and friends were well meaning, but the callow wound of infertility throbbed with each word of solace. To make matters worse, they rarely admitted to a miscarriage, an abortion, or an adoption; when they did, it was in hurried whispers with downcast eyes behind closed doors. When I took the plunge, they smothered me in, "It's all in the timing." or "Relax." The darling of the bunch was, "Let go, let God." Really? Are you fucking kidding me? He sure didn't seem to be in my corner on this one. In fact, he seemed to be sending a pretty clear all-points biblical bulletin that I was barren with a capital B. I was even pissed off at the Virgin Mary, who didn't do a thing, not one damn thing, and she got pregnant. Poof! Just like that. With my luck, the best I might expect from Divine intervention was a stigmata, bleeding from my hands, and spending the rest of my life cloistered in a cold, dank convent tower feeding pigeons.

At home in Santa Cruz, I'd tear up the sand as I walked the neighborhood beaches, scanning the horizon for an answer, a clue that might bring some relief from the insurmountable yearning and guilt. What had I done wrong? Where had I gone wrong? When had I become damaged goods? I'd spent most of my twenties and early thirties avoiding motherhood and taking all precautions. Truth be told, *I* wanted to be the center of attention. Maybe being one of eleven had something to do with it. There was always formula, a high chair, and a turbo-sized station wagon in our household. It was my Show and Tell just about every year in elementary school. It was my alarm clock. I knew I had two more hours of sleep when I heard, in the distance, the scrape of a pot landing on the stove, the whoosh of the flame as my mother heated a baby bottle.

In almost every family photograph from my tenth year on, I'm proudly holding a drooling baby boy. After delivering a perfect son and three civilized daughters, my mother unleashed four sons in rapid succession into our neighborhood, where they terrorized prized rose bushes, cats, and mailmen. The bundles of steaming tamales and platters of homemade cookies my mother sent along with apologetic note cards helped keep the police and lawsuits away, but really it was the fact she was a widow, a young green-eyed beauty of a widow with too many children, that kept our neighbors from running us out of town.

My larger than life, successful, handsome, prankster of a father died in a car accident, two blocks from our home, when I was eleven and my mother was seven months pregnant. He was plucked out of our lives just as we were beginning to get to know one another. Some things I'd preferred not knowing about him, but there were many more that made me feel grand and, most of all, feel safe. We'd lost our treasured, paternal Greek grandfather two years earlier, but when my father torpedoed to his death, it crippled us. As a family, we never recovered and have walked through life with a limp in our hearts. My father's death at thirty-eight slayed our paternal grandmother, Nana Herminia, who had only one child, and while she adored us, the mere reflection of her son's features or mannerisms in any of us would send her over an angry edge. She once railed at us with tequila breath, a machete in one hand, rage spewing, and while my sisters shielded my petrified younger brothers, even they knew it was her heartache and loneliness emerging. I wanted to avoid that kind of torment at all costs.

Maybe it was becoming a woman during the feminist movement and thinking that anyone could have a baby, but not a college degree. Maybe it was looking around at my mother, my aunts, my older sister, all saddled at home by endless demands. The only things on my horizon were career, travel, and not sharing the spotlight with anyone. Those aspirations were meaningless now. I wanted a baby and couldn't have one. I was deeply hurt and humbled.

Anyone who moves away from a large family learns that you can never step back into that family and expect to be in sync with the pack, but I knew I belonged. I shared flesh and blood, memories, and secrets that bound us forever. There's no better feeling than reconnecting with a brood of people who know you, warts and all. Now, I wanted in the most esteemed pack of all—the pack of motherhood—but the portal had slammed shut in my face.

CHAPTER II

SPRING 1993

A year after my third miscarriage, my Ob/Gyn, acupuncturist, homeopath, along with my soothsayer of a neighbor concurred my ovaries had indeed gone into retirement. The shiftless thirty-nine-year-old eggs slacking around the sacs were out of warranty. Blanks. For long periods of time I'd immerse myself in writing and work, but Mother's Day brunches and Hallmark cards always lurked around the corner.

One day I got fed up and declared no more. I'd had it. No more nudges or downcast looks for me at tortuous baby showers, baptisms, and birthday parties, where inevitably someone asked if I had children.

No more.

Give me motherhood or give me the right to be a complete pain in the ass about these two empty arms. I'm one of eleven children, for God's sake. I grew up in a town where I was related to half of the population on both sides of the border. I was entitled to raising my own after helping raise eight brothers and sisters. I was an Aries. I rammed through obstacles. I bulldozed challenges. I got what I wanted.

We decided against infertility treatments, but were clueless about the next step. Then one ordinary day, my man had the good sense to say, "Let's adopt. Adoption is just a different set of issues. One isn't better than the other."

We researched a variety of adoption options and spent gorgeous, sun-drenched weekends inside bleak conference rooms, listening to burned-out social workers while we rummaged through a bloated packet of forms or scanned the bulletin boards jammed with photos and letters with success stories. During each break I'd stare at the beaming couples cradling scrawny, pasty white babies dressed up in miniature sport jerseys or covered in ruffles and lace. I'd read their testimonials, how these tiny beings had transformed their lives, and envy would seep out of me like sweat.

A couple of months and many orientations later, we were attending the second of six adoption workshops. By now, we knew to pack our own coffee, water, snacks, notepads, pens, and all completed forms. We also knew to forget the notion of privacy. The agency had carte blanche to probe, scrutinize, and examine every facet of our lives. How often did we argue? Were we using contraception? When I penciled in that it was none of their business, the social worker rolled her eyes. To elucidate her point, she arranged our bank statements, insurance policies, credit reports, and wills across her desk much like a collage while asking us if we'd accept a special needs child or a baby conceived out of rape. Marty and I didn't hesitate—no.

We went through a series of classes with folks who had also gone through the infertility wringer. One look from them was more comforting than a slew of platitudes from well meaning loved ones. Halfway through the classes, our assignment was to compile a scrapbook about our background, lifestyle, and goals for the social workers to show potential birth mothers. We thumbed through photographs of romantic getaways to San Francisco, dancing to Annie Lennox and Talking Heads late into the night, and lingering in bed, sharing coffee and the Sunday papers, long lazy days at the beach, hiking, and mountain biking whenever the mood struck.

We'd met on Rio del Mar beach on a glorious Indian summer afternoon. Marty's jumbo-sized Golden Retriever, Astro, and two joyful toddlers plowed into me as I slept, and when I woke up startled, splattered with sand, but laughing, Marty was smitten. Fresh from a break-up, I offered him friendship and nothing more. Nothing prepared me for his goofy laugh, wicked intellect, and fun-loving persistence. A year later we were married. The world revolved around us, and few other things mattered in the heady first two years of our marriage.

Then, what seemed, like an about face, Marty came home from work and announced that one of our friends had beaten us to the punch and had gotten pregnant first.

Beaten us? First? I hadn't realized we were in a race, but instead of talking it through, asking why the hurry, or voicing my reservations, I was carried away by the rosy-pink cloud of my man wanting a child. My girlfriends, whose own husbands wanted to wait or remain childless, swooned when I shared Marty's enthusiasm. I took it as a sign and agreed to enter the racetrack. No doubt we would come in second. Then it seemed that every one of our friends, sisters-in-law, and every other woman I sighted within five hundred feet were pregnant, nursing, or toting cherubs. I didn't care if I came in last, I just wanted in.

Now the half-dozen photographs lay beside a poignant letter to potential birth moms chronicling our past heart-break, our desire to have a family, and above all promised we'd love their child with every ounce of our being. I struggled through the process of winning someone over so we could raise her child. As much as I longed to be a mother, the idea of a woman giving up a baby, for whatever reason, kept me awake nights, along with a barrage of questions. Would we consider open adoption and share our child's life with a birth mother? What if she changed her mind?

We had our fingerprints checked, scheduled a home study, took AIDS/HIV and drug tests, and not long afterward we received a phone call from the social worker. A young Latina wanted to place her child up for adoption. Our scrapbook would be one of several she'd review. Seven days later she'd chosen us as potential parents. We danced around. I cried with a full blown smile and then called our family and friends, who delighted in the news, promising to light candles and say novenas, urging us to get the nursery ready. An empty bottle of champagne remained on our night table as we held each other tight and drifted off to unfettered sleep.

That weekend we met the family of seven at a Chucky Cheese. The birth mother was a lovely, soft-spoken Latina high school student. Her exhausted-looking mother was horrified to learn, only a month ago, that her daughter was seven and a half months pregnant. The birth mother wouldn't divulge the identity of the father. The mother had her suspicions, but her daughter stubbornly remained silent. I felt sorry for both of them.

While the young girl's five siblings played in a corral of brightly colored plastic balls, we endured two hours of deafening chipmunk music. Ms. K, the social worker, yelled out questions. We yelled back our answers. I crossed my legs at the knees and ankles, leaning in to hear the mother, who did most of the talking. The shy young woman said what we wanted to hear, but her eyes failed to meet mine.

We spent the next few weeks courting the birth mother and her mother. I scrutinized every pause, cough, and hesitation, looking for doubt in the women's words and gestures. I wasn't convinced. I was biased. My formative years were molded at my maternal grandmother's kitchen table where I vied for a spot among my mother, my aunts, their friends, and my sisters to lap up the coffee and pan de dulce fueled gossip. By the time long division became important, I'd learned how women survived infidelity, illness, money troubles, and even the colossal of all mistakes, getting pregnant without the bona fide ring. Some afternoons, crisis and disaster courted both sides of the border, doubling the opportunities for my aunts who through their hilarious impersonations escalated ratty gossip into performance art. Other times, a pin could be heard as we clam shelled around the table in a stilted hush that a beautiful debutante or who would've thought, plain Jane was pregnant. You'd count the months, if they were newlyweds, but not for these stupid, easy pendejas. Every eyebrow arched, in unison, at us. I felt pinned to the back of my chair. My grandmother, Nachu inscribed the air with the sign of the cross three times, dusting her end of the table with powdered sugar from the last morsel of pastry and said, "We don't have to worry about them, they're good girls."

The bad girls' mothers took to bed, the stone-faced father either sequestered or exiled their daughter until a shotgun wedding was in the horizon. My paternal grandmother, Nana Herminia was durable wool to Nachu's shimmery taffeta and said "Only easy girls have babies before they're married." It sounds pretty tame, but you had to have witnessed the sneer and have heard the gristly syllables leave an oily 'eeeh zeeh' mark in the air. If the good for nothing coyote didn't step up, the family always did, mind you, only after the family raged and blamed each other and threatened to dismember the lowlife that had taken advantage of their little girl. Once tempers calmed, though, the family moved on to more pressing matters: guessing the gender, planning the baby shower and the baptism. The ongoing arguments would be over the selection of godparents and the perfect set of names.

This young birth mother, however, maintained her steadfast decision to place her baby up for adoption, and her mother insisted she couldn't afford to feed another mouth. A single parent to six children, holding down two jobs and not making ends meet was bad enough. That their desperate situation worked in our favor made me uncomfortable. Back at Chucky Cheese, Ms. K had cupped her hands to her mouth like a megaphone and assured them the baby would be more than well taken care of with us. They smiled and nodded. When the mother and daughter excused themselves to go to the bathroom, Ms. K looked over to me and seemed to twirl her turquoise bracelets in victory. I gave her a dirty look.

The next day I sat in her office underneath a sagging spider plant suspended in macramé. "You have to understand that most birth mothers, especially the younger ones," she paused to wave at a colleague, "change their mind a dozen times before they even have the baby. It's just part of the process." She rummaged through files with one hand while rubbing her feet with the other.

"I'm not worried about her changing her mind." I stuck my face out at her. "I don't believe she wants to give her baby up. Period. Let me talk with her alone."

"Trust me. She's decided." Ms. K straightened the miniature doll collection stationed on top of her computer. "She hasn't wavered once in our meetings. You're nervous, that's all. And that's normal, too." Her hands flew to her hair and in half a minute had an upswept hairdo secured with chopsticks. "She's due in less than a month, and by Halloween you'll be a mom. I promise. I've seen this happen a hundred times before. Ree laah kss. Just relax."

I blanched and clamped down on my purse until the overpowering urge to punch her subsided. I despised that word: relax. How dare she utter that word in my direction? Didn't she, an adoption matchmaker to a passel of infertile women, know how that one word scraped us raw? News flash! Infertile women never relax. We don't know how to relax. We're wound up tight with guilt, envy, regret, and desperation, stumbling down the only path we'll accept: the one with a baby at the end of it. Before I could give her a piece of my mind, she stood up and sprayed lavender water into the air. My time was up.

A few days later, as Marty and I were leaving her office, Ms. K gloated in my ear, "I told you so." The birth mother looked ready to explode, complained of being uncomfortable all the time, and reassured us she wanted us to adopt her baby. But I couldn't shake the uneasy feeling.

CHAPTER III

AUTUMN 1993

In early October, at three in the morning, we got the "It's time" telephone call from the birth mother's mom. I'd been out with friends celebrating an upcoming marriage with lobster enchiladas and margaritas until way past midnight. Marty brought aspirin and a tumbler of water while I showered. We held hands, smiling nervously at each other as we drove to a San Jose hospital forty miles away. Since the birth mother's cinnamon coloring and lustrous black hair diminished the possibility of a Martian-headed, bug-eyed baby, I amped up my wish list. Please a boy, not a girl, even though I'd said, all along, it didn't matter. I was afraid of raising a little girl and feeling the same way, I assumed, my mother did about me: disappointed. Crestfallen that I'd moved to another state, chosen a career first, and not given her front row seat to my marriage with a family friend's son whose thriving medical or law practice afforded me a late-model station wagon full of kids. I was terrified of making the same mistakes Mamá had made with my sisters and me. What if I was as overly critical or demanding? What if I didn't trust her to make the right decisions?

Upon our arrival at the maternity ward, we were given surgical gowns and ushered into the delivery room. My knees wobbled as the doors swung open. The intense anti-septic smell and the sight of the birth mother on the delivery table moaning in pain brought on chills that seemed to fuse my spinal cord. I closed my eyes and silently called out to my paternal grandmother and asked for strength. Could I go through with this? I felt anchored to the floor, and to Marty's credit he didn't rush me.

The memory of Nana Herminia's husky voice after long family dinners where history and life lessons were imparted, settled me: "You come from the land of Mayan pyramids and Greek temples. You have my blood coursing through your veins. Go on. You can do this."

I made the long version of the sign of the cross, as my grandmother would have, then walked over and held the birth mother's hand. I offered my support as if I had done this many times before. She crushed my hand as the doctor told her to push. She grunted and shuddered each time. I heard only the sound of my heart thundering in my chest. This was it. I would be a mother in a matter of minutes. I turned to look at Marty, who was standing behind me as the birth mother was coached on her last big push. I held my breath as the doctor held up a scrawny little girl, with a blob of dark hair, screaming her lungs out.

"Welcome to the world, Sofia Marie." Marty beamed as the nurse placed her in my arms and he held us both. The world stood still as I locked eyes with my daughter and felt her warm, tiny hand clasp my finger. There was no way on earth she'd disappoint me. I'd be her staunchest fan, applauding the risks she'd take and providing a strong shoulder to lean on when failure confronted her.

We thanked the spent birth mother. She was relieved her labor was over, but now her mother attempted to figure out whom the baby looked like. We were led to a private room where parenthood began to settle in amid the tears, laughter, and joy.

We behaved like typical new parents, enthralled by the magic of a newborn, and threw our good sense out the window. We had sworn we would be different from parents who bondo-ed their babies to their bodies and talked like The Muppets. We were worse. Every sound and movement, including bowels, was recorded via photographs, video camera, and a journal I faithfully filled with intricate details. In the middle of the night, my mom radar picked up the slightest stirring from her bassinet. Though I awoke exhausted, I was greeted with a smile that trumped my fatigue. Sofia's dark bushy hair, pixie face, and inky almond eyes were perfect. In her nursery, behind closed doors and under muted lights, mother and daughter played before getting on to the custodial needs. I'd nestle her tiny body inside my robe and hum the same lullabies my mother sang to me in Spanish before returning to bed. Life as new parents was surprisingly easy.

We congratulated ourselves one night after putting Sofia to bed, wondering why some parents made such a big deal out of everything. After opening a celebratory bottle of wine and stoking the logs in the fireplace, we had just settled down to watch a video when Sofia's piercing cries sprang us out of our cozy embrace. We ran up the stairs two at a time. We found her screaming. Fists clenched up in the air. Writhing in pain. I held her, whispering in a soothing voice while checking her diaper, the bassinet, and her nightclothes for any possible clues as the gut-wrenching wailing persisted. Nothing seemed wrong. I handed her to Marty, who rocked her as I frantically scanned through baby manuals. They were worthless. I couldn't concentrate enough to read. My mother's remedies came to mind. We burped, massaged, and sang to our daughter. She howled.

"Call your mother," I barked. Marty handed me a beet red, shrieking alien. Marty's mother was a retired nurse who had raised five of her own.

"Mom says she has gas. We need to give her Mylacon drops." He bounded back up the stairs.

I handed him Sofia and went to the medicine cabinet, cursing as I struggled to peel off the safety plastic wrapper around the cap. I placed a few drops in her mouth. The medicine turned her shrieking into crying, then seconds later intermittent whimpering and yawning that within minutes brought the glorious sound of silence. We witnessed a miracle. Tomorrow I'd draft a glowing testimonial to the pharmaceutical company and send flowers to my mother-in-law for her brilliance.

"That was awful." I gingerly rocked Sofia.

"Some babies do this for hours on end," Marty said as he fingered one of his sideburns.

"My brother's baby girl did this every night for months." I placed Sofia in her bassinet. We stood arm in arm watching her sleep. Then returned to the velvety wine as Marty rewound the video. I stoked the fire. We put our feet up on the coffee table. Threw our wool blanket over us. This time, when Sofia's shrill cry launched us from the sofa again, we knew exactly what to do. But this time the Mylacon drops didn't work. Sofia was screaming at a decibel level that had our Golden Retriever howling and running around in circles. We called my mother-in-law back.

"It's time to call the pediatrician," she said.

He asked about the formula. Our response led him to a quick diagnosis: Sofia had colic. Constipation was the villain and water would help pass her stool. In a couple of hours she'd have her bowel movement and fall asleep. We needed to call him back if she didn't.

"A couple of hours," I whined as Sofia arched her back and seemed to levitate off our bed.

"Dr. N said we should put cotton balls or plugs in our ears." Marty said.

I shot him a look of disbelief. "That's awful. You go ahead and do it. It's not that bad."

We gave Sofia water from an eyedropper as she shrieked, cried, calmed down, and wailed for an unnerving hour and a half. She finally howled and convulsed one last time as she passed her bowels and then shuddered in relief. We were amazed that a pebble-sized amount of stool could produce such violent pain. Too tired to care about the wine or video, we flopped onto the bed. Now we understood why parents made such a fuss about a crying baby. Marty nudged me. I could hear his muffled words, but exhaustion kept me from opening my eyes. He pulled the cotton balls out of my ears and kissed me goodnight.

A week later Sofia's grandmother called. My stomach collapsed with fear. Her daughter wanted some photographs. I gave her a glowing report. She reassured me Sofia was indeed in good hands.

As soon as our conversation was over, I called Marty at work. He dismissed my concerns, reminding me they had the right to call and even see the baby for another six months until the birth mother signed the consent to adopt forms. It would be all right, he repeated; it was unsettling, but not necessarily a bad thing. He urged me not to jump to any conclusions.

I called Ms. K, keeping an eye on Sofia, who twitched and smiled in her sleep.

"The birth mother is having nightmares and wants to see the baby. The sooner the better."

When I didn't answer, she continued, "It's common. This happens all the time."

"Then why didn't you tell us this before?"

"Because I've been through this dozens of times," Ms. K said and ended the conversation by imploring me to trust her and send the photographs as soon as possible. Lots of them.

A bulging packet of photographs with a letter detailing the joy Sofia was bringing to our lives went out on the same day. The rest of the week, I seized up when the phone rang and jumped out of my skin when someone knocked on the door. My body ached. I needed more sleep. Neighbors remarked at how much weight I'd lost.

Less than a week later, the grandmother called and thanked us for the photographs. She asked to see Sofia. I panicked. Surely she'd take one look at Sofia and refuse to give her up. Could I do this, if I was in her shoes? I didn't know.

"She needs to see her once. Then she'll sign the final papers." Ms. K's confidence grated my nerves.

I went into the kitchen, picked up the teapot, and was filling it with water when the telephone rang. Water spilled everywhere. I lifted the receiver with trembling hands. It was Marty, and yes, we had to take Sofia to see the birth mother. We had no choice. At first, I avoided telling my family and friends, but I needed to hear from others that it wasn't a big deal and, most of all, that we were doing the right thing. We received a bevy of responses, ranging from 'do what you need to do' to 'are you crazy? Only in California would they think this was a good idea'.

Fortunately, the visit was short. The birth mother had a bad cold and rain pelted the apartment windows. The grandmother wrung her hands as thunder rumbled and proposed we head home before nightfall. Her daughter complained, but she insisted. It was dangerous for babies to be exposed to lightning at this tender age. It could lead to blindness and deafness. I refrained from throwing my arms around the mother and said I'd been raised with the same beliefs. Not entirely true. Our superstitious housekeeper drove us crazy by covering all the mirrors and drawing the curtains to shield us from the glow of lightning. My mother would come home to find us underneath the dining room table praying the rosary in the dark.

Ms. K focused the birth mother on the album of photographs to facilitate our departure.

"There, it's over and done with," Marty, said as he drove through the Santa Cruz Mountains.

"So that's it, right? Now she *has* to sign the final papers." I reached over the seat to touch Sofia's bundled feet.

"True, but don't forget, the grace period lasts through March."

I groaned and changed the subject, but my brain remained wedged on the next few months: our waiting period. In California, birthparents had six months to change their minds. In the meantime we'd be foster parents. Why hadn't this registered before?

The next day Ms. K called to report the birth mother had loved the photo album and agreed the baby seemed happy and well cared for. Not to worry, she'd soon sign the final paperwork. Her signature at the bottom of the form was irrevocable, releasing us from this teeth-gnashing limbo. I daydreamed about the birth mother filling the space with her large loopy penmanship, my arms and heart no longer held hostage by the whims of a teenage girl. She'd have more of her own I reasoned, in time, she'd have as many children as she wanted with a stand-up guy who'd hold her hand in the delivery room, whispering encouragement while he wiped the perspiration from her forehead.

The following week, my mother and older sister, Dimi, came to visit bearing a suitcase filled with frilly pink outfits and much-needed help. They added lavender salts to the steaming bathtub, and insisted I take naps while they tended to Sofia. Every day one of my favorite meals simmered on the stove: savory meatball soup, chile con carne, and homemade chorizo wafted throughout the house. Like clockwork, right at four they brewed coffee, we wolfed down pastries, and gossiped until Marty came home. Best of all, my mother took my hand, on the third day, and told me Sofia was a very lucky little girl.

"I'm afraid," I admitted. Once the emotions caught in my throat, settled down I told her about the birth mother and the months of waiting that lay ahead. "What if she changes her mind?"

"Over my dead body," she said. The support my mother wasn't able to offer me during my miscarriages and ectopic pregnancy, she more than made up for with those four words of enormous confidence and love. My mother had survived a stroke, three years earlier, which left her right side paralyzed, but she was still a force to be reckoned with, a lioness defending her cubs in a stylish size-eight pantsuit.

On Halloween we gave out candy in a sleep-deprived state of bliss. I was frazzled, rarely showered, or dressed before noon, and pretty content. I was a mother. Life was good.

Early November graced us with T-shirt weather and the go-ahead from our doctor to give Sofia her first bath. Our friends recommended all sorts of bathtubs with brand names made up of a collision of vowels and umlauts. My mother declared that tucking Sofia in the crook of my arm was the best way to dip her into the bath.

"Just bathe her in the kitchen sink, like I did with all of you," she said. "An inflatable bathtub, indeed." My mother snorted. We decided on a small but awkward inflatable soft tub. We agreed to take turns bathing Sofia. One of us would bathe her while the other videotaped. Marty handed me the video camera and plunked Sofia into the water facedown on the tub.

"She's going to suffocate!" I grabbed him by the shoulder.

"I'm fine." Marty pulled his arm back.

"You're going to drown her." I reached for Sofia.

Marty blocked me. I could almost hear my mother laughing at us.

A festive occasion dissolved into a full-blown argument because Marty wanted to bathe his little girl. I stormed out of the bathroom like a petulant teenager not getting her way.

Later, he appealed to my sense of fairness. "You have to let me do more. I'm not a bumbling oaf, you know."

The truth stung. I knew he was right, but somehow, somewhere I had picked up on the notion that a mother's Ten Commandments included my all-encompassing veto power. My commandments left him with those duties I avoided: rinsing diapers, mixing formula, and swabbing the tip of her umbilical cord stub. Marty challenged me and became a very involved father in spite of my insistence that as the mother, I was first in line.

Much to my surprise, Marty handled Sofia's first bath like a pro. I videotaped them as she splashed the few inches of water, squinting and cooing. We wrapped her little body up in a big fluffy towel and swooned at her gummy-wide smile. She peered at us with her dark, voluminous eyes. I dried her hair into a thick Mohawk and nicknamed her Chicken Hawk, after one of our favorite cartoon characters. We laid her on our bed and gazed at her perfection. We imagined her first step, favorite food, first day of preschool, and made plans for her first birthday.

A week later I had Sofia all to myself for her next bath and was ready to show off my skills and maybe even teach Marty a thing or two, when I almost dropped her head first into the bathtub. Marty said nothing, didn't even gasp, but when I turned to look at him he was grinning from ear to ear. He'd caught it all on tape.

Thanksgiving was joyous with a newborn and the fragrant aroma of a slow-cooked meal. We took a walk on the beach and found three perfectly shaped sand dollars washed up onshore. A welcome sign. We sat down to dinner with Sofia as part of the centerpiece and gave heartfelt thanks for all of our blessings.

As the December rains created a slick mossy coating on the sidewalks, I compiled a holiday list of ordering tamales, buying tree ornaments, cookie ingredients, and toys for Sofia's first Christmas. That morning, a dear friend had delivered our daughter's first holiday gifts: a set of handmade flannel blankets and a Christmas stocking. It stood taller than Sofia. The fireplace crackled, our daughter slept in a hand strewn rocking crib, and the cinnamon smell of Mexican hot chocolate was in the air. Marty came home, earlier every day, to bundle Sofia up for her daily stroll on the beach, both of us reveling in how well the three of us fit together. It was meant to be.

By the second week of December, our families called two or three times a day, asking for more photos, wanting to know every detail and demanding we take Chicken Hawk on tour. My man and I basked in the attention and took our little girl everywhere with us, letting strangers hold and fuss over her. We beamed when people interrupted our restaurant meals and asked to see our baby girl and then remarked how good I looked. What was my secret? Adoption, I'd answer with a mischievous smile.

The day before we bought our Christmas tree, I sighed contentedly, imagining how special this year was going to be, when the telephone rang. It was the grandmother calling to say that her daughter had something to tell me. I went numb.

"Your mother says you have something to tell me." I winced.

"Yes. I'm sorry, but I want my baby back."

"Are you sure?" I flinched, regretting the dumb question.

"Yes, I want my baby back. I'm sorry."

I pleaded with her to reconsider. She only repeated the words I'd dreaded all along.

Angry, parched, and afraid of what I might say, I told her I'd call Marty and hung up. I didn't cry and wouldn't, because as long as Sofia was in my arms, I was her mother.

"What's wrong?"

"She's changed her mind. She wants Sofia back."

"Did the mother call?"

"Yes, but I also spoke with *her*. She's serious, Marty." My voice faltered.

"Fuck. Maybe it's something else? Let me call the social worker."

"What do we do?"

"Not to worry. It'll—"

"Please don't say that to me anymore, all right?"

"Sorry. I won't. I promise." We hung up.

He called back to say Ms. K was out, but she would be paged.

She called me within the hour. "Is there anything we can do?" I changed Sofia's diaper, cradling the telephone against my neck and shoulder.

"No. I just spoke with their social worker. She says the birth mother stands firm on her decision. I also spoke with the mother. They're willing to let you keep the baby until after Christmas. She was going to sign the consent papers this week," Ms. K said with a drawn-out sigh as she shuffled papers in the background. "I'm sorry."

"You're sorry?" I spat out at her. I hung up wishing I had told her where to shove her officious apology.

With shaking fingers and a dry mouth, I called Marty and let out a low moan when I heard his voice.

"I'll be home as soon as I can. I'll call Steve on the way home. Don't lose hope." I had forgotten about Marty's older brother. A successful and respected lawyer in New Jersey, who'd always made sure we knew he was there for us in case of anything, anytime. Maybe this was just a holiday depression? She'd surely call back and apologize. Wouldn't she?

An hour later, Marty arrived.

"Steve is willing to wage a war against the birth mother and her family if he has to," he declared with a rasp to his voice. "He can help us keep Sofia."

"Thank God." I said, "Did you tell him to get started?"

"No. I told him you and I had to talk first."

"About what? Call him back."

"Liz, remember what we talked about?" Marty's eyes were pained as he brought up our counseling sessions. "We agreed that if the birth mother changed her mind before the grace period was up, that we wouldn't fight to keep Sofia."

"But this is different."

"How?" Marty smoothed the hair away from my face.

"Because she's ours." I scowled, wrapping Sofia up in my arms. Maybe I'd go to México with the baby until the birth mother came to her senses. "She's willing to let us have the baby through Christmas, so maybe she'll change her mind," I said with crazed hopefulness.

"But what if she doesn't? Do you want to prolong this?"

"I can't believe you're giving up, Marty. Just like that, you're ready to hand her over? So she can live in a two-room house with seven other people?"

"I hate the thought of that," Marty raised his voice. "But we said we wouldn't fight the birth mother for the baby. We wouldn't want to tell Sofia when she asked about her birth mother that we had the money and where-withal to fight for her. We agreed we wouldn't go there. It wouldn't be fair. Right?" Marty's voice cracked as he flung his head back against the headboard and cried out in agony.

I covered my ears and violently shook my head as a profound rage and grief stirred deep within me.

The phone rang.

"Don't answer please. Not yet."

"It's not going to change anything." Marty kissed my forehead and answered. "I'll call you right back," was all he said. He sat back down on the bed and took my face in his hands. "We agreed, right? We can do this, together. We're Team Santa Cruz, remember?" His watery hazel eyes filled me with a maddening despair. I caved in and nodded. He walked downstairs slowly as I rocked myself, praying that I'd wake up from this ghoulish nightmare.

I could hear him talking on the phone. Then his heavy footsteps marked his arrival as fading sunlight cast long, ominous shadows across our bedroom. The twisted look on his face told me what I didn't want to accept. I curled my body around Sofia and sobbed.

He draped his body around mine. "I'm so sorry," he whispered. "I never truly understood when you miscarried or had the ectopic. I didn't get it before, I'm so sorry." His body quaked as we wept.

We spent the next forty-eight hours cocooned in a debilitating sorrow. When the time came, I walked from room to room, picking up Sofia's belongings, which had once been scattered throughout the house. Sofia slept as I collected her handmade flannel blankets, tiny buttery-soft moccasins, musical toys, and her guardian angel. I walked into the living room and saw Marty sitting outside on our deck, slumped in grief as rain spilled over him. He was soaking wet. My heart wrenched at the sight of my husband defeated. I made a move to bring him in, but something stopped me, made me give him his time. I sat waiting for him with a batch of towels and a steaming teapot. When he finally walked in the sliding glass door, he let me undress him.

"I didn't know this kind of pain existed," he said.

At ten o'clock the next morning, we clung to each other and sobbed as we watched Sofia coo, gurgle, and kick her legs at us when we laid her on the agency crib and said good-bye.

We spent the holidays sequestered. For months I slept with a letter I'd received from my oldest brother, Peter. He'd gone to church and lit a votive candle to help my tears and grief flow. His anger kept him from praying to God. Instead he'd prayed to our grandparents, asking them to do him a favor, and kick God in the ass when they saw him. What would I do, if I came face to face with God? Walk away was my answer. I had nothing to say to him.

CHAPTER IV
JANUARY 1994 TO MAY 1995

Losing Sofia unraveled us, stripping me of my sense of humor and compassion, exposing an electrically charged mean streak lying dormant deep within me. Our outlook on life soured, it turned callous and cynical. Family and friends became strangers. We were lost within our community and spiraling out of control without a safety net. Scorched earth. Annihilated. Nothing looked or felt the same. Webster's dictionary didn't have a word to describe the jagged, oozing, haunting pain, so I retreated. I imploded and spoke to no one, besides Marty, for the first three months after losing Sofia. My mother, who after eleven children, bless her, doesn't remember anyone's birthday and rarely calls her children, actually called me, indignant that I hadn't called her. She left me a taunting phone message, but I didn't take the bait. How could she empathize, I reasoned. She, the mother of all mothers, who'd set a record in our hometown hospital, had become a grandmother at forty-one and here her daughter couldn't hold on to one.

I carried such a raging torch of anger that Marty was left alone to confront the world. The scab-removing questions took a toll on him. We were pissed-off juveniles aching for a fight ready to rip apart any conversation and reveal it for the shallow crap it was, because nothing, absolutely nothing, came close to losing Sofia. NOTHING.

By mid June we'd sold our home, closed our businesses, stored our furniture, packed up our car with the bare necessities and camping equipment, then drove away from our life. It was an escape and adventure infused with sadness. We crisscrossed through Yosemite's high sierras down to Mt. Whitney, pausing to hike countless trails until exhaustion trumped our afflicted thoughts and granted sleep, fitful at best, but a welcomed respite. I made a detailed list of our favorite campsites, hoping to return, some day, and savor the sounds of flowing rivers, birdsong, and majestic granite beauty. A week later, we drove through Death Valley in the middle of the night, to avoid the peak temperatures of the hellish furnace, where we passed glistening joggers, I was certain, were nothing more than a desert mirage.

By July we set up camp in Oak Creek Canyon outside of Flagstaff, Arizona, and frolicked in the cool thin layer of water cascading over smooth swaths of lichen-stained rocks. The solitude seemed to massage the anxiety from our muscles, but amplified the sense of being untethered. Our search for a camping hammock became the day's purpose. It led us on a day trip to Sedona, home of the Secret Red Rock Mountains, a burnished crimson masterpiece highlighted against a deep blue sky. Maybe we'd hang out here for a while? After deliberating for hours and purchasing a hammock, we settled on lunch at a restaurant with a bird's eye view of the water-sculpted pinnacles. Watery salsa arrived with bright green and red tortilla chips.

"You've got to be kidding," I said to Marty.

He pointed at the wall hanging of a raunchy sleeping Mexican under a saguaro.

"Let's find another place to eat." I threw my napkin on the table.

"Nope, let's order some beer."

"In that case, make it tequila." It felt good to laugh. We made plans to explore the area as we ate our lackluster meal, but when we left the restaurant, pink-and-white striped canopied jeeps zipped by, advertising spiritual vortex tours with goofy white guys sporting Native American headdresses at the wheel. We retreated to our campsite.

The one constant in our life was music, blaring from our car speakers, alleviating the sadness for brief moments, as we lost ourselves in soulful U2 lyrics. We no longer danced with wild abandon or slow stepped, locked in each other's arms. We were in mourning, our bodies keeping vigil.

While I anticipated the Fourth of July pit stop in southern Arizona with my family, I girded myself for the inevitable: the next generation. Last year I'd daydreamed of our Chicken Hawk huddled within the pack of newly hatched nephews and nieces, forming a tight bond with her cousins. My man and I in the fray of comparing baby gadgets, contributing our comical missteps, and turning to my mother for advice. I'd salivated years for that moment, but as soon as I set foot in my mother's house with my backpack and not a bundle of joy, my flight response kicked in. After a boisterous welcome, I ferreted for Sofia's photographs in my mother's living the hallway, and her bedroom. They'd been put away to spare our feelings.

My siblings gathered, I doted on my nephews and nieces, praying my lighthearted façade remained intact, but once we exhausted our camping stories, my brothers rehashed their jokes, and my sisters conceded on refashioning my look, the visit proved awkward and forced like a TV sitcom with a laugh track. No one brought up Sofia.

My mother, a night owl, kept me abreast of the family gossip late into the night, the two of us alone, sharing her bed while polishing off her stash of butter cookies and See's Candies. The few times we brushed up against intimate conversation, I was certain she'd at least allude to Sofia, but when fatigue won over, I kissed her goodnight.

"Mijita, do me a favor," my mother asked on my way out the bedroom door. "Reach into my top drawer." She pointed to her dresser.

I pulled out Sofia's silver-framed photograph, my precious little girl smiling back at me, and clutched it to my chest. Without a word between us, we embraced and wept. When I finally went to bed, I placed Sofia's photograph among the other family portraits and thanked her.

Two days later, we headed northeast to Santa Fe. Once there, my dearest and oldest friend, Ana, comforted us with her savory meals. I immediately spotted Sofia's photo on her refrigerator door as Ana made me laugh with her own brand of dark humor. She led me on long walks under expansive, sapphire-blue skies, where I unleashed my pent-up sorrow, and like a much-needed salve, she asked me about Sofia. I didn't have to tuck her away and band-aid my gaping wound around Ana. I cherished those moments more than she'll ever know.

In August we flew into the touristy, air-conditioned resort town of Ixtapa, in México, but settled a few miles away in hot, humid heavy Zihuatanejo, a sleepy fishing village. Swimming, snorkeling, and exploring the quaint town occupied our days, but at night I'd bolt up drenched in sweat, suffocating under the gauzy mosquito net. My ritual was to drink a glass of cool water after reassuring Marty to go back to sleep then wait for the slightest sound of pitter patter and shine my flashlight around the ceiling and corners of our open-air palapa bungalow until I'd spot the transparent green geckos flitting in and out. If sleep still passed me by, on merciful nights, I'd devour half a book or douse my journal with ink and sweat. I'd torture myself with what if, should have, and could have scenarios. Then, as if to push the knife through the threshold of my pain, I'd summon sweet morsels of our time with Sofia and smile before the piercing sting of reality slayed me. Was my little girl safe? Was she loved? Did she miss my voice, my touch?

During our second week Marty bought a soccer ball and sprinted up and down the long fingernail of a beach, dribbling while I wrote letters and read stacks of books. People stopped to stare at his endless set of skillful drills, which he stopped only when drenched in sweat to drink water and plunge into the ocean before repeating the process. A couple of days later, while we stocked up on crispy rotisserie chicken, creamy fresh cheese, and fragrant melons and mangoes in the main market, two affable, but fast talking guys recruited Marty into their soccer team. They'd seen him working the ball from the open-air restaurant on the beach, where they worked, and were thrilled I spoke Spanish. They needed players. It wasn't a joke, they promised, and pleaded with us to attend practice that same evening. We went. Marty suited up and stunned them with a succession of goals in the first half. I wished I could contain the unadulterated glee on his face. I'd forgotten he could smile like that.

They practiced and played barefoot on the town's main beach, where the sand felt like white-hot barbeque coals, propelling the players to the water's edge, whenever possible, to keep their soles from blistering. It seemed half the town attended, even though they were held in the middle of the afternoon, cheering the team and jeering the opponents when they scored. Marty's teammates nicknamed him The German because of his no-nonsense style of play and steady stream of high-impact goals that helped lead them into the playoffs. I was grateful for the sense of purpose it gave Marty and afforded me a temporary distraction from my empty arms until the crowd of women with their children teased out the tentacles of overpowering envy, bordering on resentment. Marty, it seemed, focused only on setting up a play or receiving a ball launched overhead a cadre of defenders, noticed my crossed arms and pinched expression. We'd lock eyes or, if time permitted, he'd pass by, find my hand, and squeeze it.

The day of the final match, most of the businesses closed for the afternoon. The pompous mayor and a sultry Miss Corona, in a modest one-piece bathing suit and glittery sash, presided over the festivities and jovial crowd. The popular beer company sponsored the playoffs, so their signature blue-and-yellow banners hung from every street lamp and palm tree around town. I no longer had to wedge myself through the crowd for a place to watch the game; instead the team manager parked me front and center with the other families and presented me with an honorary parakeet-yellow *Restaurante Rossi* jersey.

The team won a hard fought championship, and we were paraded around town on the back of an oversized pickup truck while the players hoisted the gargantuan gold-plated trophy into the air. We ended the night with mariachis serenading our feast, and after what felt like never-ending shots of top-shelf tequila, these lovely people begged us to stay and put down roots. We were tempted, but Oaxaca City beckoned. Our last week in Zihuatanejo, folks recognized us everywhere we went, young boys asked for Marty's autograph, and delighted restaurant owners waved away our money and asked that we not forget them.

We thrived in bustling colonial Oaxaca, where I photographed elaborately painted doors, archways, and windows, or scoured the markets for textiles while Marty polished his Spanish and learned to read and write. I spent entire afternoons browsing through bookstores and fell in love with contemporary writers who served up an honest and wickedly funny portrayal of Mexican high society and their infatuation with anything American. We hooked up with a fun-loving group of Americans studying at the Instituto

Cultural with Marty. They insisted we speak Spanish at all times and hailed me as queen for my flawless Spanish.

"But you don't speak Spanish with an American accent?"

"How's that possible?"

"Mexican mother," I answered. "From Sonora."

"What does that have to do with it?" One of the guys said his Latina mother forbade Spanish.

I explained that my mother, even after living in the United States for over fifty years, refused to renounce her citizenship and proudly touted her green card until President Clinton told her, via television, that it was time she came into the fold. She demanded formal Spanish in her presence. Drawn-out saucy bits of slang like *¿que paso, carnal?* or *nel pastel* were reserved for friends and never left our lips once we stepped through our front door. I elucidated how she stopped conversation to correct the slightest grammatical error, in front of anyone, and when it came to the written word, she edited our letters, written to her, with a red pen and enclosed them with her response. I nodded when they called her fastidious and pompous. They understood.

I also regaled them with stories of Mexico's golden years of cinema, kept them away from tourist establishments, and requested obscure songs from mariachis playing in the zocalo, garnering our group a round of amber-colored mescal from the locals. We bonded during excursions to Zapotec temples, mescal distilleries, and remote dusty villages where weavers and woodcarving artisans invited us into their homes. But late at night, when arm in arm, they headed to the discos, my man and I fell out of step and disappeared in the opposite direction. By late October 1994, when preparations for Día de los muertos were in full swing, we confided in two friends who were curious as to our plans for a family. Fortified by shots of mescal, we recounted the loss of our daughter while we walked back to our apartments late one night, as wiry stray dogs escorted us from one neighborhood to another. They listened as we traversed cobblestone streets, all of us by now, used to the smell of bus fumes and dim lamplights casting wobbly shadows. When we were done they gave us the gift of cussing out the birth mother, her family, the adoption agency, and the fucked-up result of our noble intentions. We hugged. I sobbed until my heart ached and a nasty bout of hiccups made me call it a night.

On the Day of the Dead, we spent the day going through the city visiting homes and businesses that opened their doors to show off the intricately decorated altars paying homage to their departed loved ones. I'd watched my maternal grandmother, Nachu, refresh flowers, and light tall glass-encased candles in wrought-iron stands inside her little chapel situated behind her Spanish stucco home. She'd genuflect in flickering candlelight before kneeling on the wooden pew, as rosary beads trickled one by one through her fingertips. Her face tilted upward in supplication to the Virgen de Guadalupe who crowned her altar, her susurrations remained a mystery to me. My paternal grandmother, Herminia, had a wall-to-wall wooden altar in her bedroom adorned with church-sized saints, an anguished-looking Jesus on a massive cross, who seemed to watch over the array of votive candles and flowers that weren't given time to wilt. This altar did double duty and also served as a camouflage where my grandmother, a restaurant owner and businesswoman extraordinaire, stashed her money, jewelry, gold coins, and important papers in a heavy-duty metal safe housed underneath the starched white linens.

But nothing prepared me for Oaxaca City's tradition of erecting and embellishing three and four-tiered altars wrapped in ornate garlands of delicate papel picado and crowned with brilliant orange marigold and blood flower arches. They spent days cooking and laying out bowls of mole and banana leaf-wrapped tamales, fruit and nuts arranged into works of art, bottles of favorite beverages alongside their loved ones' photographs and mementos. Each family member set out ceramic skeleton figurines in a variety of poses and dress, sugar skulls of all sizes next to a trail of shimmery goblets of water that acted like a beacon of light to show their loved one the way home. Bakeries made special Day of the Dead bread, ordered days in advance, to ensure their altars were complete with loaves decorated with skulls and crosses made of white icing.

On November 1st we toured the city from dawn to dusk, taking in everyone's uniquely glorious altars and stories. We asked for permission to take photographs and the gracious folks of Oaxaca were honored. Since then, I've created our own altar and still show off the photographs, every year during Día de los muertos, and have lovingly named the slide show *Altarcation*.

At nightfall we joined a procession of noisy costumed merrymakers taunting the Grim Reaper as they wound through town and spilled into the main cemetery lit by hundreds if not thousands of candles where families gathered around tombstones to pay their respects in a bittersweet tradition accompanied by food, prayer, and music.

Out of respect, Marty and I sat on the cemetery wall, keeping our distance, mesmerized by the open display of sorrow and suffering. I wept with them. Later that night, my eyes landed on a row of tiny mounds of dirt, each punctuated with a small white cross and candle, all flanked by a huddled family. A sliver of hope, like a jagged piece of broken coral, ascended and pushed against the tidal wave of anger and despair. At least Sofia was alive.

By early December, as promised, I called a longtime friend from Santa Cruz, that now lived in Cuernavaca, an hour or so away from México City, and who found us an apartment in her neighborhood. Marty played with her young son, as her husband was away on business a lot of the time, and Evy and I talked for hours on end. Watching my man inventing games and roughhousing with her little guy was painful at times, but he seemed more at peace at the end of the day. We explored the labyrinth of a city and walked everywhere until exhaustion led us back to the tranquil garden surrounding our temporary home and the company of good friends.

The festivities leading up to Christmas were mercifully low-key: no Frosty the Snowman or Silent Night on the radio or in stores, no Christmas tree farms or decorations, no holiday list or gift buying. Instead neighbors opened their homes for evenings of conversation, games, and served a hot fruit punch and crescent-shaped cookies. Some folks gave out small paper bags filled with oranges, nuts, and hard candy shared by all. While we cooked Christmas dinner, I stood over my dear friend while she disinfected and picked out miniscule slugs from a head of romaine lettuce, a leaf at a time.

She leaned in and said, "You were meant to be a mother, you know. Marty and you are so good with kids." I rested my head on her shoulder while tears streamed down my dress.

Was I? Meant to be a mother? I no longer believed that.

During the second week of January 1995, I woke up in the middle of the night with a throbbing pain in one of my molars. The next day, after examining my tooth, a dentist gave me painkillers and recommended my dentist follow through right away. We jumped at the chance to go back, even though I knew in my gut that this was the end of our escape.

We decided to return to the States, hunting for a new place to settle. New Jersey or Arizona? After four months of testing the waters for jobs and homes closer to family we felt like Goldilocks: desirable New Jersey towns felt too small, too cold, and Arizona cities seemed too big, too hot. During the end of our stay in Phoenix, on a lark, we attended an Internet tradeshow in Las Vegas to learn more about the World Wide Web, which was taking off and, like the Wild West, up for grabs. We bought spiffy new clothes, had our hair styled, and set off for Nevada, where Marty was hoping to find a niche. After three non-stop days of amassing information, we headed back to Arizona on blasting-hot Highway 93. While we reminisced about our travels in México and the global connection of the Internet, we came up with Electric Mercado, an online portal of Latino commerce, literature, and culture. The idea settled our sense of discombobulation. We decided to relocate back in

Santa Cruz, but not without some trepidation. A week later, atlas in hand and, much to my family's disappointment, we said bittersweet good-byes to answer the sixty-four thousand dollar question. Could we re-enter life and set roots in Northern California?

CHAPTER V
SUMMER 1995 TO SEPTEMBER 1997

We arrived in Santa Cruz with a new sense of appreciation and approached our small town with a lens of curiosity, taking nothing for granted and enchanted again with sunsets on obscure little beaches and bicycle rides through neighborhoods canopied by stout maple trees. We made a pact to avoid falling back into old ruts and habits; instead we'd make time to visit bookstores and art galleries, we'd maintain our daily exercise regimen, and pause in our day to people-watch over coffee or a beer with the same enthusiasm we'd had traveling in México.

Friends welcomed us back into the fold, excited to hear about our adventures, catching us up on life and gossip, but thankfully skirted the topic of children. I'm embarrassed to admit that I selfishly didn't reconnect with all of our friends—those who had babies, toddlers, or were in any stage of pregnancy were off limits. I'd rather undergo a root canal sans anesthesia than withstand the stories, photographs, and videos of their baby's head crowning while a sage midwife coached them at home, in their bathtub, to the sounds of Enya or Kokopelli flutes. The thought of watching my friends with their kids, up close, mortified me. It hurt, and I don't mean my feelings. It physically hurt, like a scalding bucket of water thrown on me. I'd feel sunburned for days. Give me time, I'd plead with Marty, who finally threw his hands up in the air and grew used to me ditching him whenever there was a family sighting. He'd stay to congratulate and fawn over our friends' kids, pretending I was somewhere else, and promised that we'd get together. Soon. Soon equaled never. No way. No how. When I'd reappear with a flimsy excuse, he'd scowl and tell me he hated lying to our friends. My apologies were wearing thin.

Deep down inside, though, I didn't care if our friends felt slighted. After one cautious visit or two, I knew the powerful floodgates of motherhooditis would give way. I'd come back from México tanned, fit, with a resolve to create a new life, but beneath my brittle veneer, nothing had truly changed. Why did I have to sacrifice my feelings, I reasoned, just to be polite? Marty countered that I couldn't keep running away and hiding from life. Oh yeah, says who? Somewhere along the way, I'd cloaked myself with this rationale: my hideous suffering had earned me the right, like a warrior's trophy, to pick and choose, include, exclude, and limit those friends who were fortunate to have a healthy reproductive system. They could have children, but not my friendship. Now, I look back at that time and shudder at my coarse attitude. My gracious and loving friends never held it against me. When I was finally able to reemerge, years later, I placed the blame squarely on my shoulders and told them it was all about me. A woman gone over the deep end by the loss of a daughter and a dream.

When we finalized plans to start our online commerce and publishing site, we needed to get serious about our living arrangement. Childless friends had all opened up their homes to us and were in no hurry for us to leave the party atmosphere that prevailed long into the night, but we were itching for our own nest. After several days of scouring the rental ads for one- or two-bedroom houses we either couldn't afford or that stunk like a fraternity house, we took a break. Then we relented and called a real estate agent and toured houses, where they inevitably fussed over the extra room for a little one, a sappy smile aimed at my direction. Time out. Exit stage left. I'd wait for Marty out in the car. It also didn't help that the locations sucked: traffic noise, lawns littered with sofas, cars jacked up on blocks, butt-naked surfers changing their attire out front.

By the end of the week, a Walmart-sized argument catapulted us back to square one. Stewing in traffic, we spotted a large for lease sign at the Old Sash Mill Complex. Work/live studio lofts were available in the historic, hip, mixed-use commercial community, walking distance to downtown. A couple of hours later, grinning from ear to ear, we signed a one-year lease on a tiny, two-story studio in the newer part of the complex flanked by friendly architects, graphic designers, and various other entrepreneurs.

Within weeks we'd established our dollhouse-sized bedroom and bathroom upstairs and had rummaged through our storage unit for an old set of tall bookshelves to divide our workspace in the front of the first floor while the back half was devoted to our kitchen, dining, and living rooms. It felt good to set up house with our lamps, rugs, and artwork, sleep on our own linens, and cook with our pots and pans. After a string of fits and starts, we bought computers, printers, scanners, and office supplies and began attending hi-tech mixers and Chamber of Commerce breakfasts, but maintained our promise to exercise and take time out for friends. Using our bikes for transportation and living lean suited our tight pocketbook and well-being. The heavens seemed to align when two key folks, with freelancing gigs to make ends meet, eagerly signed on to help us create the look of Electric Mercado and gather content. We recruited gung ho UCSC students for internships and plunged into our dream. At the outset, long walks, friends, and fun were peppered throughout the week to balance out the steep learning curve of this unknown frontier. Within months, six-day, eighty-hour workweeks, and stress canceled life outside those four walls. We hadn't cracked the code on how to make money and not deplete our meager savings. Internet sales and paying advertisers were few and far in between, folks were leery to purchase online, and credit card fraud was a fast-growing enterprise.

It didn't take long for the balance to be tipped against us. The Internet craze, the competition to be first, whatever the heck that meant, and desire to be an outstanding, award-winning, attention-grabbing site with a myriad of technical bells and whistles kept us working long into the night. Most times, we weren't aware of the weather: sunny, foggy, rain, a drizzle, or torrential downpour, even though the studio's entire front wall was a floor-to-ceiling window.

Our hard work paid off, days after our online launch, on September 15, when a major San Jose newspaper surprised us with a stellar review for our savvy, creative, and artistic Latino marketplace and publishing house. The phone rang non-stop, we granted radio and television interviews, won numerous awards, presented at major Latino Internet conferences, and rode the wave of accolades, but for the life of us we couldn't figure out how to translate that into dollars and cents. Money headed in one direction—out—and when it did come in, it was a trickle.

We sent our regrets and didn't join our families for Thanksgiving, Christmas, or New Year's Eve while we struggled to earn a living until Marty took a full-time position as Director of Internet Services at a local company. He reasoned he'd float our boat and glean the leading-edge technology while on the job and get us paying gigs designing the company's multiple Web sites. It made sense. We celebrated our good fortune.

But with this new routine, the fuse in our relationship sparked, and the tension escalated exponentially. Marty came home, after a full day at his job, to take over the technical aspects of the Web site and worked late into the night. My background in education and publishing hardly prepared me to code HTML or troubleshoot technical issues. Marty gave me quick and dirty tutorials while I scribbled and smudged copious pages with notes, flow charts, and never ending to do lists until I began to grasp the basics, but soon his response to my unrelenting questions was *RTFM*. He'd give me an evil thin-lipped smile and turn back to his mountain of work. I had no choice, but to *read the fucking manual*. Dense reference books covered in black and white sketches of animals, an ostrich, or platypus that read link an index of footnotes. I was petrified full time. Pride muzzled my insecurity. Admitting shortcomings was unacceptable. Plus an overachieving tendency to load up on whatever came my way discharged an overbearing attitude and further strained the already threadbare connection between us.

The upside of my days, however, was conversing with writers, musicians, chefs, and visual artists around the world, who gave us permission to reprint and sell their work online. A big sister at heart, I kept our colleagues and interns fed, soothed frayed nerves, and coaxed them over challenging Web site design issues with music and a non-stop pot of strong coffee. Four hours of sleep a night, an evening out, or a relaxed meal was a luxury.

Family called, but they got used to our quick talks and empty promises, except for my mother. Upon hearing, from my sisters, that we'd be absent at Easter and Mother's Day, she called as I sat hunched in front of my Mac proofreading the Web site, periodically giving orders via gestures to interns at nearby desks, while my mother gave me a piece of her mind. A protracted piece of her mind.

"Elizabeth Anne."

When she realized I wasn't listening, she lowered her accented voice, repeated my full name, and with measured words reminded me whom I was speaking to. Then she told me how much she loved me and choked up. I rolled my eyes at the receiver, but deep down inside, I was a sucker for her attention and practically cooed back.

"Mijita, you're working too much. How are you ever going to conceive again?"

"I'm not."

"Of course, you will. Leave it in God's hands."

"Good idea."

My mother didn't catch my sarcasm and continued with her patent lecture mixed in with her favorite sayings and some Catholic cheerleading. As soon as I could, I seized upon some ratty bit of gossip and changed the subject. I imagined her stirring sugar and evaporated milk into her coffee, the daily newspaper spread out in sections beside her. To her credit she never asked me if I was pregnant, but every pause in our conversation seemed like it should be backfilled with baby related words. A long walk up to the university or a martini at the end of the wharf, or both, was necessary to shake off the stress and my mother's disappointment.

Soon after, a ferocious and truculent fight forced my man and I into counseling with our dear and longtime therapist who listened then brought us to our senses and sent us on our way with homework. For starters, we had to separate our work relationship and our marriage, we had to keep a journal, go on dates every week, and take time off from work as individuals. A firm taskmaster, our therapist insisted we report our progress and accepted no excuses if we slipped off the wagon. We were in serious trouble, she said, and she didn't want us to become a divorce statistic.

Though Marty had been raised to think that therapy was some kind of new-age bullshit, to his credit we spent months hashing out our feelings, learning guided imagery, and crafting sand trays of the vision for a life together. We painfully picked through our past, one deliberate step at a time. It took over a year, but we found each other again. The passion and profound love we had for one another was unearthed, and while life was not perfect, we knew our life together was unshakeable.

CHAPTER VI

OCTOBER 1997

Out of the blue, the morning of our ninth wedding anniversary, Rick, my brother's brother-in-law, called us with an offer to help us adopt in México. A dashing young priest whose mission in life included serving those in need, particularly children in his El Paso, Texas parish and in orphanages across the border in Ciudad Juárez. My four hours of sleep were a walk in the park compared to Father Rick's utter devotion and duty to his calling. Of particular concern to him was DIF, Procuduría de la Defensa del Menor y Familia, an agency similar to Child Protective Services. They also housed children until reuniting them with their families or placing them for adoption. His enthusiasm and positive outlook were infectious.

We'd met Rick at my older brother's wedding seven years earlier, the same wedding I'd been ejected from by my ruptured fallopian tube. He'd led a dance floor full of guests through the latest line-dancing steps and surprised everyone when he and a handful of his best friends conquered the dance floor with their hip, choreographed moves. My younger sisters had a crush on the handsome charmer who seemed made for a tuxedo or leather jacket instead of a clergy collar. At family events, you'd find him in the center of a group, while shoulders around him leaned in to hear every word, laughter erupting. We'd often debate about the church. The machine. His patience with our cynicism was humbling.

"How are you feeling?" Rick's voice calmed my coffee-fueled jitters.

I gave him a brief update on our start-up with a touch of the latest family events and a bit of humorous gossip. We traded stories before he went on to the first order of business.

"Do you think you're ready to try adopting again? One of the orphanages might consider you as possible candidates." He was direct.

"We've actually been working on the paperwork for an international adoption," I said.

"You're kidding? That's great."

The conversation felt providential. We agreed to wait for his next call.

I quivered at the bubbling of hope, awkward and unfamiliar, surging through my body. We insisted, though, on acting subdued. Stoic. Neither of us admitted that maybe we'd done our penance. Perhaps, we'd been absolved for our patience.

We replaced the memoirs and novels on our nightstands with stacks of books highlighting the benefits of adopting children from Latin America, Russia, and China. I toyed with the idea of joining a support group, but chickened out after attending a meeting where a husband and wife team, in matching Disneyland T-shirts, led the circle of couples in a long-winded prayer, followed with pronouncements about the right countries to adopt from. I snuck out before the break.

As always, our family and friends jumped on our band-wagon and it seemed everyone now knew of someone who had adopted and would love to share their information with us. The motherhood portal seemed to unlatch and reveal a heady mix of joyful hope and promise.

Less than a week later Rick called us with good news— we had an October 30th appointment to meet with the director at DIF. Marty had to pry me off the ceiling. Visions of a dark-haired beauty crawling around our home paraded in front of my eyes as I tried, in vain, to concentrate on work.

The day before Halloween, Rick navigated his car from El Paso across the border into Ciudad Juárez. The early morning sun stenciled weak rays of light over the smoggy city. The sprawl looked like most border towns, with massive billboards peppered among the new buildings that butted up against filthy crumbling ones. Impoverished indigenous people roamed the littered streets swathed in shawls, trying to sell their trinkets and nurse their young.

Throngs of beat-up buses and taxis competed against late-model BMWs, Cadillacs, and SUVs, which seemed to rule the streets. We slowed down upon entering the ragged industrial end of town where DIF's office resided amid a large abandoned construction site. Rick parked the car in front of a decaying building, laughing at our baffled reaction.

"Only in México, no?" He filled our hands with boxes of baby and medical supplies while cautioning us the parking lot was littered with shards of glass. Long tendrils of rebar jutted out from unfinished concrete walls neighboring the non-descript building with a hand-painted black-and-white DIF sign. The front entrance, while dreary, was free of debris, and the glass double doors served as a bulletin board announcing upcoming meetings and classes. The hit of Pine Sol flipped my stomach as we stepped through the doors, avoiding the patches of wet floor. In the far right corner, an older gentleman wrung a dingy mop. At seven forty-five in the morning the lobby chairs and back wall were occupied by a mass of people facing the receptionist behind a fort-like counter. All eyes shifted to us. I focused on the drab green walls decorated with posters of family togetherness then tipped my forehead and smiled at the families who didn't look away. Rick introduced us to the receptionist, who let the phones ring as she gave him her full attention. When she rose from her chair to introduce herself, Recepcionista, as she preferred to be addressed, stood maybe an inch or two beyond four feet, but the beehive hairdo and disco stilettos gave her an extra twelve-inch advantage. Marty nudged me. I'd been rendered speechless by the voluminous eyes topped with broad brushstrokes of jungle-blue eye shadow, licorice-whip eyebrows, and meticulous tangerine lips. Her firm handshake rattled the cuff of gold bracelets. Low-riders and flamenco dancers came to mind.

By nine o'clock most of the people in the lobby had met with one of the social workers. Some walked back out within five minutes clutching papers, their eyes haunted. When our name was called, we followed a social worker and re-entered the world of interviews, forms, and psychological evaluation exams. This time it was all in Spanish. Marty feared we'd be shown the door or he'd be placed in a strait-jacket once they scored his test.

His enthusiasm for learning Spanish and embracing our culture had endeared him to my family from day one. My mother and my New Jersey husband would discuss politics and the latest family crises over afternoon coffee. My mother, giddy with pride, coaxed him to finish his sentences, and dismissed his grammatical errors with a wave of her manicured hand. When I, hands on hips, complained, she chided me. He wasn't a native speaker. He's not one of your daughters, I'd think to myself, and would leave the room pouting.

At DIF, he impressed Ms. H, the psychologist, during the oral interview with his eloquent answers. Back in her office after a break for lunch, I winced when she showed us the results: Marty yielded a score of superior intelligence while my results were only above average. (He hasn't let me forget this, but promised not to tell my mother.)

After the testing we entered the nursery, a large rectangular room with a carpeted sunken pit the area the size of a small swimming pool, where eighty-plus children, ranging from toddlers to teenagers, spent the day with precious little to do.

The second we walked through the double doors, every single child, as if on cue, turned our way. The noise settled down from one corner of the pit to the other. Some of the kids smiled, some looked away, others stared, but the older girls approached us.

One of the girls asked about my citizenship when I greeted them in fluent Spanish. They eyed my clothes. A doe-eyed beauty with a swollen, stitched-up lip gently touched my earring, and the leader of the pack snatched her hand away, reminding her of her manners.

"You speak Spanish well, for a gringa." They giggled.

"Gracias." I told them my mother would be pleased by their compliment.

"Do you want a boy or a girl?"

When I said it didn't matter, they eyed me with what seemed like suspicion.

"Do you want an infant or toddler?"

Before I could answer, they pointed out the favored candidates. Those toddlers didn't cry much and had light curly hair. A couple of the girls trotted off and returned with fair-skinned babies.

Surreal. These young girls knew their chances of ever being adopted were slim to non-existent. When we asked them questions, they politely stated the rules unless, of course, we wanted to adopt them. Their eyes held hope.

An older girl, a few yards away, seemed to be massaging a toddler's small head.

When I asked her what she was doing, she answered, without looking up, "lice," refusing to make eye contact or conversation with me. In a far corner of the room a group of older girls each attended to a baby while little boys ran around playing with and fighting over broken toys. With fierce determination they protected pieces of plastic and metal and wailed when they were left empty-handed.

We wandered into a large, stifling-hot sleeping room filled with rows of metal twin beds on either side. Toddlers everywhere—crawling, walking, crying, having their diaper or clothes changed by women who consoled them and played with them for a few minutes before needing to go on to the next one. The room smelled of soiled diapers, sweat, and baby powder. We held the little ones, who wailed when we put them down to pick up another. How did one choose? Were we going to choose? Was I holding our child and didn't know it?

We progressed from one step to the next and returned a week later to good news. We'd been placed on the prospective parent list and assigned a dainty little social worker who explained the adoption process and then gave us The List: a menacing legal-sized sheet of paper with thirty requirements, all vying for attention. Each document had to be accompanied by an apostil (a certified seal and signature ascribed only in Sacramento, California) and translated by a certified court interpreter. The bitter news was the waiting list for Mexican citizens was six to nine months, and since we were Norte Americanos the time period could easily double. The knot in my stomach tightened; I was afraid I'd choke from disappointment. We smiled back and thanked her as our hopes for a quick adoption were dashed. Why did I let myself get hopeful? When would I learn?

We shuffled back to the lobby where Rick was waiting.

"At this rate, I'll have dementia and forget I ever wanted babies," I said.

"And I thought I had some pull." Rick put his arm around Marty. With his usual optimism he said, "Let's have hope. We'll talk to the director."

From the corner of my eye, I noticed a couple walk in with two toddlers and another couple walk out, triumphant, carrying their chubby, grinning baby boy.

We remarked on every movement in the lobby. A door opened a slice, for just a few seconds, and it served up a cornucopia of small talk. Waiting. More waiting. We shared the last cold Coke from the vending machine and worked ourselves into a froth of indignation and impatience.

A man in a business suit approached Rick as we huddled next to the water cooler. The following hour is still a blur, but according to Marty and Rick the man overheard our plight and, in impeccable English, offered his story. He and his wife, who was seated in the corner with the toddlers, were returning them after only two weeks.

Marty identified them as Americans and said, "We're screwed." Americans had a reputation for returning adopted children. I focused on the woman, who looked older and seemed tense, while the boys sat next to her holding hands. A blessing to have a juicy distraction from the endless waiting. I scrutinized every inch of her, every movement, her lacquered hairstyle, pastel outfit, and tried guessing her age. Fifty? Hands folded in her lap. No purse to be seen. Then her husband joined her. He tucked the boys around him. I looked away with envy. A few minutes later the four went into the director's office. Rick talked. Marty paced. I looked for another distraction and settled for the next set of shoes walking through the front door.

An eternal hour and a half later, the director ushered us into her office, apologizing. She'd only have a few minutes with us because of an emergency situation that required more of her attention. Rick apprised the director of his side conversation with the gentleman and assured her of our staunch commitment. Marty snorted. I rehearsed my plea while she put up her hands to stop us. She'd spoken with the social worker and the psychologist. I sucked my gut in. Held my breath. Rick offered a short prayer. Marty clasped my hand.

The director told us about the challenge of adopting siblings. Most families, like us, wanted one child, preferably an infant. This couple had been in counseling for a year before deciding. Her eyes trained on Rick. This was a huge blow to the staff and the children that they'd back out of their commitment. Rejection stampeded right at us. Again. Tears stung the edges of my eyelids. Rick gnawed at his lip. She asked us to please hear her out before we said anything. Marty raked his hands through his hair. I crossed my arms in defense. I wouldn't wince when motherhood slammed shut in my face. Maybe we just weren't supposed to have a family.

The director inquired if we were willing to take two weeks and consider adopting the toddler brothers who had just been returned. We couldn't answer now. We had to go home, talk to family and friends, and call her in two weeks. Just like in the movies, in dreamy slow motion, I felt thrown into the deep end of an icy pool surrounded by bubbles obscuring my senses and judgment.

Two? Did I hear her correctly? Two boys. No little girl? No baby.

Marty and Rick gathered me up in their arms to celebrate. Without our knowing, the social worker and the psychologist had thought we were a perfect match and moved us to the front of the line. I could be a mother in two weeks. Two weeks, not a year! We could be saying grace at Thanksgiving as a bona fide family.

The next thing I remember crystal clear is Agustín, at three and a half years, introducing himself with a firm handshake before collecting his little brother. I scooped up a congested, feverish Ricardo, who had a serious respiratory infection. Marty was giving Agustín a piggyback ride to a private room where the four of us could hang out. I took several tissues from one of the day care ladies and wiped the poor little guy's nose when Ms. D, the boys' social worker, showed up with a sour look to accompany her pantsuit, long straight hair, and heavy makeup. She didn't approach us, though, and huddled with the director and psychologist. Rick discreetly remained close by the trio.

"Are you thinking what I'm thinking?" Marty nudged me. I turned to see his eyes shining. I nodded. "This is divine intervention."

Finally, I'd crash Mother's Day with someone else's babies, who'd never in a million years be mistaken for our flesh and blood. They'd lucked out. These brothers didn't have my husband's beak nose, my bad teeth, or olive-green skin. I figured I'd disinfect and perfume them, put them in Old Navy outfits with flax-enhanced Fritos in one hand and an Odwalla juice in the other. When the boys opened their mouth and Spanish tumbled out, I could envision myself with a Mona Lisa smile, confirming they were among the chosen elite at the coveted "Los Amigos" school. I'd brag my geniuses lapped up calligraphy, Mayan math, yoga, and sign language.

No more hiking to remote, off the grid hot springs or desolate waterfalls to escape the most dreaded time of the year. I'd have my status back. My title would be reinstated: mother. I wouldn't feel excluded. I'd have my rightful place at the table when the women in my family or friends huddled, to top each other, with their kid stories.

Hours later, the three of us were in bumper-to-bumper border traffic crossing back into El Paso, talking over each other about the incredible change of events and our impressions of the boys. Rick brought up the only uncomfortable part of the afternoon that Marty had not witnessed.

"Well guys, Ms. D thinks you're too young to adopt the boys," Rick teased.

"Well, I'd like to thank her for the compliment." I postured. For once I wasn't considered an older mother-to-be as most forty-four-year-olds were.

"But the biggest obstacle she has is that you're gringos," Rick added as I caught his grimace in the rear view mirror.

"She actually said that." Marty cocked his head.

"No, she was polite. She said *norte americanos.*"

"Well, we're just going to have to win Ms. Prickly over," I said, not wanting to let anything spoil the day. When we reached the border crossing, the inspector asked us what we were bringing back from Ciudad Juárez. I couldn't help but say, "hope."

CHAPTER VII

NOVEMBER 1997

November 12th

Dreams were vivid. In one I'm hiking up a steep trail that turns into a sheer cliff, which forces me to continue to the top. I'm petrified when I look down and see the shore and water so far removed. I want to be on land. How did I get here? I keep repeating to myself. I reach the top and find it dangerously narrow. I don't know how to get down.

In another dream I am happily pulling our huge naked baby in a wagon. Baby is grotesquely ugly, huge deformed head, face full of pimples and a mouth full of permanent teeth. I don't care. It's our baby. I am hauling the baby around in a jumbo-sized Radio Flyer wagon for the world to see.

By now we knew the boys' father had left before Ricardo's birth. The mother supported the boys by herself, working all day and night, while the boys fended for themselves. The neighbors had heard the boys' relentless crying and tried to help, but found the apartment locked and called the authorities. The police and a social worker from DIF had found three-year-old Agustín taking care of his baby brother. They took the boys to DIF and left a written notice with instructions for the mother.

Ms. H, the psychologist, then went on to tell us that the mother had shown up a few days later with the requested documentation for Agustín: a birth and baptism certificate. She'd told them she didn't know her husband's whereabouts. They enrolled her in parenting classes and offered financial assistance. She saw the boys before she left, but never returned. Why not? It didn't make sense to me. Mexican women didn't abandon their children. They might leave their abusive husbands. They'd leave their homes and possessions, but not their children. They'd rather live on the streets begging for food than abandon their own. Had she been a victim of the serial killer who'd been stalking the city for over a year? What had kept her from returning? This haunts me still.

Years later, when Agustín entered first grade, I kissed him on the cheek and whispered I love you in Spanish before leaving the classroom. He looked pained, but said nothing. I chalked it up to first day of school anxiety. Weeks later, when I did the same thing, he asked me, after school, what "te quiero" meant. Puzzled that he didn't recognize the endearment, I explained. His entire body exhaled, and he said he'd always thought it meant good-bye. A big smile crumbled as he wrapped his arms around me and wept. Were those the last words he'd heard from his mother?

Ms. H then escorted us to the director's office where she ended our meeting with good news. We'd received provisional custody to take the boys to a hotel in Juárez for two days. I'd taken a risk and packed each of them a small suitcase with wheels filled with new clothes, books, and toys.

As Agustín unpacked in the hotel room, he asked several times if the items were theirs. Forever? Ricardo had a bronchial infection with mucus coming out of every orifice in his head, but he still smiled and played, with his big floppy head trying to catch up with his tiny body. Marty and I stayed up late watching them sleep.

When the boys woke up the next morning to play, we discovered they'd hidden their toys behind the floor-length drapes so that no one would take them. We swam, played, wrestled, read, napped, sang, and went to the park during our forty-eight hours together.

Sunday evening arrived unwelcomed. The staff had to intervene and gently help us pry their warm little hands from our arms and clothes. We promised them we'd be back. Soon. They cried. We promised. They wailed. Memories of losing Sofia surfaced. Fear rode shotgun. The mother could come back. The father could reappear. The grandparents, godparents, uncles, and aunts could all come forward and take their beloved little boys home, where they rightfully belonged.

November 17th

I woke up from a nightmare that Agustín and Ricardo had cried themselves to death. I called DIF and they reassured me that they were both all right. I don't believe them and call Rick and ask him to please visit them as soon as he can.

CHAPTER VIII

DECEMBER 1997

We arrived at DIF five days before Christmas and found the clothes, shoes, and jackets we'd bought for the boys were now on different children. At first I bristled, then guilt swayed me when one of Agustín's friends ran up showing off her new Mervyn's T-shirt and tennis shoes her mother, she said, had dropped off for her. Agustín sported a mishmash of clothes with a belt so long; he tripped on it as he walked. He didn't seem to care that someone else had his clothes.

We whisked them away to the hotel, filled the tub with bubble bath and rubber toys, and made fun of each other as we went through several rolls of film in the bathroom alone. I studied them while they ate, slept, and played. Agustín, without fail, shared his food, drinks, and candy with Ricardo. If we pulled out a toy for him, he asked if we had one for his little brother. They still hid their toys behind the drapes and underneath the furniture even after we reassured them that no one would take them.

On the second day the hotel phone rang as we napped. Marty picked up a water glass and then the alarm clock before locating the phone. Ms. D, the boys' social worker, had good news for us. Marty jotted down phrases while he asked questions. He underlined some of the words.

Ricardo stretched out his pudgy arms and smiled the second he saw us next to him on the other double bed. I beckoned with my finger. He rolled off the bed and I helped him climb into ours. I tucked him into my body and covered us up with the blankets. Agustín continued to sleep.

"First the not-so-good news," Marty said. "DIF can't grant us an extension for our custody permit because we haven't been approved as foster parents yet. But, we might have a good chance of getting a special visa called a humanitarian parole from INS to get the boys home for Christmas. Ms. D says this is a good time to get one, since it's a holiday. If we're lucky we can get a two-week visa."

"So why are we waiting until tomorrow?" I opened up my blanket and let Agustín slip in.

"They have to prepare the documents first," Marty explained. "I know what you're thinking, but there is no way we can do this before four-thirty. Let's not do that to the boys."

I conceded feeling buoyed by the new possibility. "Look, a family burrito," I pointed, giggling at our threesome and then opened the blankets once again to let Marty join our bundle.

"A super burrito!" The boys squealed with delight as he enveloped us.

Hunger drove us out into a bitterly cold, windy evening. We had dinner with Rick, discussed our plans for the next day, and toasted to Christmas with the boys in California.

The next day we bundled up the boys in their new jackets and dropped them off at DIF with the promise we'd get dinner together in a restaurant again. Agustín smiled and hugged us. Ricardo wouldn't cry if his older brother didn't, and the brave little guys didn't shed a tear as we left the nursery and strategized with the director and Ms. D.

They explained the document we were after, gave us a sheet of paper with the words "Human Tar Ion Payroll" at the top with an address, and wished us luck. The director promised we could leave for the airport the minute we had the humanitarian parole. We zeroed in on the main Mexican border crossing and presented our document at an obscure counter located on one far side of a vast lobby constructed entirely of marble. We held hands, attempting not to look nervous. Our request was denied within minutes, but we were handed a sheet of paper with some scribbled words. We headed for a building called Gobernación.

"Now this makes more sense," Marty's spirits lifted as he opened the big double doors and saw the building directory. Within ten minutes we'd hit another dead end. The employees took pity on us and asked everyone in their department, but no one had ever heard of a humanitarian parole.

We returned to DIF and were ushered into the director's office, who was shocked we'd returned empty-handed. After numerous calls and side conversations, we sped off to the smaller border crossing where the social workers had struck pay dirt in the past obtaining special visas during this time of year. It took us longer to find a parking space than it did for us to hit our next rock wall.

That night, back in El Paso without the boys, we drank our dinner as Rick gave us another bit of hope. An immigration lawyer, knowledgeable about humanitarian paroles, had returned his call. He thought we had a solid chance if we could get an appointment with an INS officer first thing in the morning. Rick warned us that hundreds if not thousands of people were after the same thing during the holidays.

An hour after dawn, armed with our portfolio of documents, we entered the massive INS building and were given a number. Before long, a giant of a man in a sky-blue suit with a Santa Claus tie, informed us, with great care, it was impossible to grant us a humanitarian parole since the boys weren't in a life or death situation. We stared back as the bad news sank in.

"Look, México is concerned you would take the children to the U.S. and not fulfill your obligation to adopt them. End of story. I'm very sorry." He shook our hands and led us back out to the hallway, where he nudged us towards the exit sign.

By mid-morning we returned to our hotel room, where I dove under the covers, in my clothes, while Marty made a dozen phone calls.

"Hey, come on. We have one more chance and it's a good one." Marty's enthusiasm energized me to wash my face and try again.

We crossed back to Juárez and convened with Rick and Ms. D at the American Consulate, where armed soldiers thoroughly checked our bags and called ahead to the central office to confirm our appointment. We passed a series of nondescript buildings, commenting on the absence of lines weaving out of the entrances. We took this as a good sign. Rick opened the heavy metal door to the last building in the compound. We entered a large room buzzing with activity. We took a number and stood in a corner, where we rehearsed how we'd present our case.

Ms. D, in her impeccable navy blue pantsuit and pearls, would go first, make the introductions, and present the director's letter encouraging the embassy to grant us permission. Marty would follow, explain our situation, and request permission to take the boys home for the holidays. Next Rick, who wore his white collar for added effect, would recommend his approval. I'd make the emotional appeal last. While we perfected the most important points I erupted into laughter. Ms. D and Rick stared at me in disbelief. Marty took hold of my shoulders. I looked up at him and laughed until I doubled over and tears streamed down my face.

"What's so funny?" Marty asked.

I tried to catch my breath, but I'd only laugh until my body shook. What I really wanted to do was throw a fit and rage like a maniac. Our life had become a three-ring circus of paperwork, agencies, and lines. We had become beggars.

Marty asked me again. A purple vein appeared across his temples. They called our number before I could answer.

I registered their collective look of panic. Ms. D dug tissues out of her purse. Rick, with eyes to the ceiling and lips moving, made the sign of the cross. I willed myself to stop laughing. After a series of deep breaths, I blew my nose and motioned for them to go ahead.

We managed to articulate our case in the precise order we'd practiced while the gentleman listened to each of us. He smiled, thanked us for our brevity, and left. No one said a word until he returned. Smiling. Placing our file in front of him, he clasped his hands, leaned forward, and said, "I am only authorized to give Father Rick permission to take the boys to El Paso to be in his care while you, Mr. and Mrs. Picco, stay at his home with the boys. Is that possible, Father?"

"No, I am leaving for Arizona tomorrow to spend the holidays with my family," Rick answered. He looked at us, "I'm so sorry."

"But we'll stay in El Paso," Marty offered.

"We only want to spend Christmas with our sons," I added.

The administrator apologized, reiterated the rules, and wished us a merry Christmas. After a depressing lunch where I resisted the impulse to down shot after shot of tequila, we slapped on a good face and went to spend time with our sons.

My attitude changed the moment our sons ran over to us wearing another ensemble of clothes. Agustín's slacks were at least twice his size while Ricardo's lavender top with a glittery ballerina barely fit. I'd foolishly labeled each new item of clothing with a permanent marker as if they were attending summer camp. How gringa of me.

"Papi, Papi," Agustín yelled from across the length of the pit as he jostled through a knot of older kids blocking his way. He tripped, pulled himself right up, and stumbled again. He dove to the floor, maneuvering through their legs; miraculously he didn't get stepped on, and popped up on the other side. Marty scooped him out of the pit. He stunk like moldy sauerkraut. His feet swam in a pair of camouflage tennis shoes. If these two little boys could live among a swarm of children without knowing what the hell was going on from one day to the next, I could stop whining and take up the battle for my sons like La Malinche and conquer the bureaucracy until we traversed the border.

We had arrived back at DIF as the children were preparing to attend a Christmas party sponsored by Motorola, in their company cafeteria, for several orphanages in the city. They'd sent a bus to ferry the children and staff. I was touched by their gesture, but wasn't fond of their track record. I knew about *las maquilas* as a child when Motorola constructed one of its first foreign factories outside Nogales, Sonora's city limits during the mid-1960. In 1997 Motorola was one of over three hundred foreign-owned factories in Juárez responsible for employing 175,000 workers, most of them earning poverty-level wages, and also dumping mass quantities of toxic pollution into the environment with the tacit approval of the Mexican government. The EPA and OSHA don't exist in Juárez. I kept my opinions about the factories to myself and concentrated on the boys.

The old Yellow Bird bus filled up as we closed windows and reminded the kids to stay in their seats.

"I wonder if they've used this bus before?" I said.

"Why?"

"Well for starters, the dashboard and windshield aren't decorated. Where's the Virgen?"

Marty laughed.

"I'm not kidding." I looked around for the bus driver.

"You're right," a voice said behind us.

I turned to face a young social worker whose expression mirrored my concerns. I had no clue she spoke English.

"Where's his license? It's supposed to be below the dashboard on the right." She stood, scanning the front of the bus.

The bus driver appeared looking haggard and disoriented. He plopped down, started up the engine, grinded the gears, and sped down the street before anyone had the option to question him.

"Hold on." The staff yelled out as the bus approached the first red light. I handed Ricardo over to Marty. We sandwiched Agustín between us, sliding down in our seats in seeming preparation to plummet down a roller coaster.

The bus driver slammed on the brakes. The head social worker admonished him to slow down. He nodded at her every word and apologized with a series of yes, madams. When the light turned green, he sped off again and drove straight into a series of gigantic potholes that catapulted us into the air. The boys landed on top of each other, giggling. The kids were enjoying the ride and mayhem. The rest of us were mortified when he turned left at a busy intersection and careened onto the middle lane, horns blaring at us. Somehow we avoided a collision.

We arrived at Motorola in one piece, in part, thanks to the hum of prayers heard throughout the bus, and were greeted by a group of employees wearing Santa Claus hats and huge grins. They ushered us into their cafeteria, where Christmas decorations, a sparkling tree, streamers, balloons, and blaring rock en Español completed the festivities. We sat down at tables where a mass assortment of rainbow-colored junk food and candy appeared by the trayfuls. The kids stuffed their mouths and slurped down neon-colored drinks through blinking straws as they bounced around the cafeteria. Agustín looked bewildered. I stuffed Ricardo's ears with tissue paper and covered his ears with his cap.

"Poor kid. He's so congested," Marty said as he wiped his raw stub of a nose.

I imagined my mother and mother-in-law admonishing our decision to take him out anywhere, given the freezing weather. Marty and I took turns with our little one out in the hallway, where the noise decibel was bearable.

The employees mingled with the children, making sure they had plenty of hotdogs, pizza, and drippy nachos to eat before they brought out the cake, ice cream, and stockings filled with candy.

An hour later, as the kids' shrieking reached a crescendo, the pulsating music stopped. The shrieking didn't. A huge clown sprang out of nowhere burping, telling off-colored jokes, and honking his horn after every punch line. He encouraged the kids to burp along with him until one of the boys threw up on his big floppy shoes. Finally the gifts and stockings were handed out to the children, and one of Motorola's directors offered us one of their drivers to take us back to DIF. We thanked the employees and wished them all a peaceful holiday.

The four of us rode back in silence, arms intertwined, knowing that our time together was almost over. The last flight, at eight thirty that night, forced us to leave. We told the boys how much we loved them and promised we would be back soon. As we hugged Agustín good-bye, his thin body went limp. He sobbed. My heart broke. We repeated our promises and love for them, hoping, like a salve, our words would comfort them until our next visit. The four of us held on to one another until the staff insisted we let them go. Marty and I left knowing our sons would cry themselves to sleep that night.

CHAPTER IX

JANUARY 1998

We marked the New Year by heeding our therapist's advice and took an entire week off from work. The fragile scab-like balance in our work/home relationship was strained, even more, with the adoption heaped on top of this unlit pyre. It was luxurious to sleep in, but awkward when Marty reached under the sheets to caress my back and neck while HTML littered my concentration. Instead of pulling his warm body toward me, I'd hesitate, remembering petty annoyances or his gruffness earlier in the week. His tender persistence paid off, dismantling my scoreboard of unmet expectations, and in turn I responded to his hands and arched toward him. Our dear friends plied us with great food, wine, and conversation. When the poor souls casually asked, "What's new?" our relentless barrage of stories and dissections of bureaucracy must have bored a hole in their cranium, but, to their credit, they poured more wine, asked more questions, and hung in there with us.

Even our most sincere efforts to regain our old lifestyle seemed futile at times as we buckled under the intense pressure of another start-up, more aligned to Marty's background, and the adoption process. My man, who dreamed of being an astronaut until, at age seven, an optometrist confirmed his colorblindness, likened our pathetic attempts to a spaceship skipping off the earth's atmosphere or burning up in re-entry.

By the end of the week, though, glimpses of our past touched our middle-of-the-day naps and lovemaking. A long-forgotten, silly joke made us laugh then guffaw until we rolled around holding our stomachs, like old times. That same night when I choked up over the spots in my vision and my acute fear of cataracts, Marty took off my glasses and cleaned them. I couldn't help but think of my father, who'd done the exact same thing with my pair of turquoise, cat-eye glasses after I'd come home from elementary school squinting. Now, Marty ran warm water over the lenses and frames twice to remove the layers of smudges and crud. I cried from relief when he replaced them on my face. I saw the clarity of his love.

Having a regular life, whatever that meant, became an all-consuming preoccupation. Our longing to have our children home transformed the last phone call of the day, my last thought each night and first one at dawn. Agustín's anxiety, Ricardo's health, the next visit, the paperwork, and the upcoming hurdle all percolating at once.

January 12th

> *Dream was gross and unsettling. I was peering into a mirror and found a huge zit on my chin and when I squeezed it, it squirted out long strands of gunk that seemed endless. A miniature version of myself stood on my cheekbone and pulled on the strands until I fell and was covered by the mess.*

At the end of January I visited the boys alone while Marty conferred with potential investors in New York. We'd promised Agustín and Ricardo we'd return at least once a month, every month until we all went home together. I took a suitcase heavy with books, jigsaw puzzles, jump ropes, clay, crayons, paper, and scissors for the kids in The Pit.

Rick and I arrived with a car full of provisions from his El Paso parishioners and the staff flitted around him, carting packages and chatting. A young social worker led me to the psychologist's office.

"What a pity he's a priest." She sighed with disappointment. While I agreed it was a shame he was out of circulation, I never pitied him in the least. Rick loved his parish, working with his congregation, and creating a huge family of love and care on both sides of the border.

After a brief meeting with Ms. H the psychologist, I bee-lined into the nursery and found The Pit not yet overrun with kids. The bulk of them were still in the cafeteria finishing breakfast. Not a sign of Ricardo, but Agustín was twirling around in a corner when I scooped him up and whispered how much I'd missed him. The rancid smell made me hold my breath for a few beats. Was it spoiled milk and Lysol? The whole building had a strong odor of disinfectants, huddled bodies, and a lack of ventilation, but the kids, being kids, reeked. He looked up beaming and held onto me, but didn't say a word or answer my questions. I didn't press him. His pals gathered around us as they filed out of the dining room. Agustín reared up, scowling, and batting them away with his foot until I whispered into his soft earlobe, "I like your friends, but I love you and Ricardo." He remained tense and sullen.

The kids formed a tight circle curious around us. "Are you his mother?"

"Yes." Agustín nuzzled up against me as his friends traded smiles and nudges. A little girl with wispy braids and missing teeth informed me her mother was due any minute. One by one they mentioned, how at any moment, a father, mother, grandmother, or aunt was coming for them. Each one interrupted the other's story. Eyes darted towards the double doors when they swung open, hoping a familiar and loved face would rescue them. I listened as my throat tightened with sadness.

A little hand pulled on the back of my hair as I heard a hoarse giggle. Ricardo extended his arms to me, but Agustín refused to budge. The social worker placed Ricardo on my lap after I asked Agustín to help pass out boxes of crayons, paper, and clay. The kids gathered, but didn't reach for the supplies. When I pulled out construction paper and crayons, with a magician's flare, it got the older girls' attention and they slid their fingers across the bright colored paper and sniffed the crayons. Some of the girls sat cross-legged without the babies in their arms, giggling behind their cupped hands. Others splayed out on the stained opaque carpet drawing big hearts, writing their name, on pink and purple paper in flowery cursive, or playing Tic-Tac-Toe.

"Do we have to share these?" The girls asked while holding bundles of crayons or colored pencils in a tight fist.

"No. Keep the box. Put your name on it. I'll bring more next time." They cut strips of paper and fashioned them into elaborate three-tiered paper chains while they whispered among themselves.

Ricardo dug his fingertips into a dense block of red clay. I tore off a little piece and handed it to him. In exchange I received a slobbery kiss. He rolled his tiny hands around a piece of clay until a red dot appeared on the palm of his hand, then disappeared into his mouth. I swapped a book for the clay. Drool would be a part of everything Ricardo did while he was teething and on the hunt for anything chewable.

By mid-morning, we were in our private room, with a two-way mirror. The psychologist explained that she, the director, and the social workers would observe us. I was to draw the brothers out and interact as much as possible for the next hour and a half. Agustín drew scratchy long lines in browns and blues then explained to the mirror and me as he pointed that this was his first mom cooking three fried eggs and his dad driving away in a big white truck. I don't know if he saw something in my expression or expected more of a response from me, because he marched over to the play kitchen and showed me, with great detail, exactly how his Mamá had them breakfast every day. He placed a plate with three plastic fried eggs in front of me and proceeded to tell me that as soon as his Papá was done, he left in his big white truck.

I asked Agustín the same set of questions about his drawings for years. He always replied with the same short list of memories of a happy home. What happened to his father? What made him leave? No one at DIF knew.

Not much later, a comforting aroma of fried tomatoes, onions, and chicken broth wafted from the industrial-sized kitchen. We lined up to wash our hands in the large communal bathroom where the dense odor of disinfectant and sewage made me lose my appetite. The bathroom was clean, but the plumbing was a disaster. We followed the line into the dining area inside the sparse kitchen where Agustín joined his friends at a large table with benches. I placed Ricardo into one of a long line of high chairs. The staff served each child quickly while admonishing them to sit still and demonstrate proper table manners. As soon as the meals were all served one of the cooks led the children in saying grace.

Ricardo slurped each spoonful of soup I touched to his lips. A sullen little girl on one side of Ricardo stared at her soup while a curly-haired boy sitting on the opposite side dipped his fingers into the bowl and squished pasta between his fingers before dropping it to the floor. I looked at the rest of the children in the high chairs. There wasn't enough staff to help feed them individually. Some of the children pushed their bowls away, sending the bowl and its contents flying to the floor. I flashed back to my childhood where meals with my siblings required eating with one hand while helping a younger one eat with the other. I picked up a spoon in each hand and took turns doling out soup to Ricardo and his pals, who rewarded me with big juicy smiles. Halfway through the meal, I prompted Ricardo to grab his spoon and copy my actions. He did. We clapped to his success while some of the soup dribbled down his chest. I walked over to Agustín, who was taking enormous bites out of his ham and cheese sandwich and gulping a lime-green drink from a tall plastic tumbler. I gently pushed his hair away from his huge almond eyes. I asked if he liked his lunch. He nodded then gave me his sandwich and opened his mouth. I fed him and then put the tumbler to his lips as he swung his legs in delight. He drank without holding on to the glass.

After lunch the psychologist escorted us back to one of the private playrooms. While the boys played, I recounted to Ms. H the torture of returning the boys to the nursery after our visits. What if they stopped trusting us? Ms. H took my hand and said that our visits were extremely important. Agustín understood.

I disagreed. A four-year-old shouldn't have to understand.

She replied with a compassionate look. We shouldn't lose sight of the positive aspects of our visits. When our observation time ended, Ms. H informed me that Ms. D, the boys' social worker, wanted a word with me. I cringed. Though a fierce advocate for Agustín and Ricardo, she disliked the idea of two Americans becoming their parents.

Ms. D waved me into her office as she straightened a pile of file folders then tossed a clump of paper clips into her desk drawer. The shared office with two other social workers was tiny and cluttered, but her compact desk was a masterpiece of organization.

I pulled up a chair and initiated small talk about Santa Cruz and Juárez. Ms. D looked up, with a clothesline of an expression.

She cleared her throat. "Ricardo's ear and respiratory infection are not getting better. This is after two rounds of antibiotics. The night staff told me he's having high fevers and more earaches."

"The mucus seems worse," I agreed. "Is there anything we can do?"

My questions were answered with cryptic words and little eye contact.

"Thank you for your extra efforts with our sons."

She looked up and cracked the color on her lips to utter two words, no more, no less: "Así es." Loose translation: it is what it is. She was done and with two words dismissed me. I'd come to resent those two little words as much as I despised the sight of government buildings and bureaucratic rubber stamps. In my fantasy, I upended her desk as she shrieked, horrified, and apologized profusely. In reality, I was afraid to make her angry. Afraid she'd make a case against us adopting the boys, but I found I couldn't stand up.

"Why don't you like us?"

Her face met mine. I waited for her explanation and apology.

"I don't trust norte americanos—they are frivolous."

I caught my breath. She didn't hem and haw or hesitate. Nor did she apologize. She sat there staring at me, triumphant, it seemed, that I had asked the question.

When I took too long to answer she said, "Así es." She stood up to signal our meeting was over. I didn't stand up. I remembered my diminutive Nana Herminia, strong as ironwood, stood up to condescending businessmen, who underestimated and chided her for running the front end of the restaurant business. I somehow channeled her courage.

"We adopted a little girl five years ago and gave her up when her birth mother changed her mind. Do you think it's easy taking another risk like this? The frivolous couple that returned the boys were Mexicanos. Not Norte Americanos." I could sense my grandmother's pride at my succinct and tearless speech and sat up straighter waiting for the chink in her armor to appear.

It didn't. She didn't even blink, and I wondered if she'd been listening at all. No apology, no condolences over losing Sofia, merely an "Así es."

I stormed out of her office and back to the nursery. I spent the rest of afternoon with the boys in a small playroom, on the floor with them. At the end of the day, Rick joined us. The boys mistook him for Marty, and as they jumped up to hug him, they stopped themselves and looked at me.

"Tío Rick," I said. The difference sunk in. It was time to say good-bye.

Agustín was angry and unresponsive. I promised to return. Rick took him by the hand as I carried Ricardo, taking slow, deliberate steps to their sleeping room. I kissed Ricardo's cheeks and hands while I put him down on their twin bed. My tears plopped down around him. Agustín relented and hugged me when he realized Rick and I were indeed leaving. When we were at the front door, I had a sudden urge to go back inside and see Agustín. I did and found him wandering around the nursery. When I went up to him he didn't respond with excitement at seeing me again. He didn't throw his arms around me or smile. I kissed him on the forehead and told him we would return. He just stared as I talked.

CHAPTER X

FEBRUARY 1998

The only redeeming quality about February was the lack of a twenty-ninth day. The soggy month passed without a visit to the boys. Worse, we'd made no progress with the adoption petition. Our phone calls to the orphanage were fruitless. The social worker was out in the field. The director was in a meeting. I left messages, not expecting Ms. D or anyone to return my calls, but overworked, harried Recepcionista did call, offering apologies laced with thin bits of news from the quagmire.

"The petition is most likely buried in a mountain of files. You'll be lucky if someone reads it by the end of next month. I'm so sorry."

When I choked on my thank you, Recepcionista kept her tone even and said, "God willing and the Virgin overseeing, those boys will be with you in no time."

I hung up, grateful for her words, but my frustration mounted into a metallic anger I could taste in the back of my throat. Our petition wouldn't be read for at least a month. Thirty more days heaped onto this nightmare.

As someone who'd been baptized both Greek Orthodox (my father's side with a big party after I was dunked) and Roman Catholic (my mother's side, done in secret), I took her update as a sign. An omen. A bleak one. Maybe this wasn't meant to be. Maybe we were supposed to have only one child at a time. Maybe it was meant to come out of my body. On occasion I'd find myself leafing through the fertility section of the yellow pages, picking up the phone, and dialing, but I stayed one beat shy of ordering a battalion of hormones to help us conceive. I'd hang up riddled with guilt and shame. Afraid to admit to family and friends I was having second thoughts. Afraid to admit, to myself, that I couldn't take on two kids. Everyone meant well, when they assured me if anyone could do it, we could. To make matters worse, Marty absolutely believed I could.

A couple of times when, after a martini, my chin would quiver with the weight of my feelings, a trickle of courage edged me forward. Now! I'd scream at myself. Tell him. Go on! Tell him how you really feel. He'd sit forward, and while I fortified myself by gulping the rest of the drink, he'd beat me to the punch and confide how dismal things were at work. The extraordinary push to get his company's digital broadcasting product ready for a Las Vegas tradeshow seemed futile when tiny problems mushroomed and everything that could possibly go wrong did. Computers. Clients. Equipment. Contracts. His fear of failure and our dwindling savings kept him up nights.

I'd hold his hands. Relieved on one hand, because I was a coward, but mostly I was pissed off at myself for holding back.

After months of eighteen-hour days, six days a week, I was the perfect host for a nasty virus and was dispatched to bed. A couple of weeks went by before I could stand upright and face the sun. A violent cough kept me from talking to the social worker or the boys. A high fever wiped out all thoughts of agencies, deadlines, persnickety embellishments, raised seals, and a long single file of poufy signatures awaiting our required documents. For the first time in months, I indulged in sleep and dreamt of what I most wished for in the world: to be pregnant.

In my dreams, I was fit, showing, and mother-magazine radiant in a hip earth-toned maternity outfit with a youthful hairstyle and a stylish backpack. No diaper bag for me. My dreams showcased the pregnancy I never had the chance to have. Me, swimming at four months and eating tubs of ice cream. Me, assembling a sustainable wood crib, at seven months, a crooked smile splayed across my chubby face. My favorite: me barefoot, and waddling around at nine months. I even dreamt I had a toddler and was thirteen months pregnant in another. A colossal relief to wake up from that one.

I complained and whined about being sick, but was slyly grateful. Sick equaled sleep. Sleep equaled dreams. I could carry on a divine affair with a fetus: a second and third trimester pregnancy. It was luscious. My dream world whisked me away to a brief but gold-leafed past. I'd gotten pregnant before. Three times actually, but never made it past the first trimester. I miscarried twice and the third time a weathered and spent fertilized egg ran out of steam on its way through my right fallopian tube. Like a firecracker dud, it didn't blossom into a baby, but had enough power to blow through my tube. Messy. Very messy.

The intense desire to turn my body into a factory never waivered, I just didn't vocalize it any more.

Usually an illness plagued me with fitful, debilitating sleep, but not this time. Now, it was restorative. Powerful. Sleep came easily with extra-strength cold remedies and piles of blankets and pillows. I fell into a deep slumber where I reigned center of attention in sunny, well-appointed, but messy homes strewn with award-winning children's literature, thick non-toxic crayons, plush blankets, and a trail of stuffed animals. The colors were soft and hypnotic. I was intensely visible. A community project of sorts where everyone voiced their opinions about the pregnancy while I beamed touched by their concern. I became connected to people by merely displaying a bulging belly and announcing a due date. Everything I did was noticed, commented on, and my family called me all the time. In my dream I had great tousled hair, rosy cheeks, a touch of fine wrinkles, and wore pashmina pajamas. My daily dreams served up a taste of each month, where I'd catch a grainy glimpse of our baby on a sonogram in one and stave off morning sickness in another, leaving Saltine crumbs on my rustic Mexican bed.

Then the dreams evaporated. Just like that one night, I was no longer able to spin gold. The portal to my escape vanished and the only other visible door flickered in the distance. Upon opening it, stress dreams poured out. Bureaucracy. Entanglements. Empty arms. Work. Gigantic zits. Missed deadlines. My reality.

As a dingy February ended, we caught up to Ms. D. Normally, I bit my lip while she droned on and on about the two inches of progress we'd made and the miles left to go in the bureaucratic process. This time she began the conversation with an update on Agustín and Ricardo.

"Agustín is not listening. The staff complains that he's acting like an American brat," Ms. D informed me.

I bristled. American brat? This was also part of the drill, getting her dig in. Something anti-American, something subtle, but I wouldn't let on that it hurt. I didn't dare react. Wouldn't give in and let her see me sweat. She had no clue who I was. I'd show her.

"Ricardo is responding well to the treatment for his stomach reflux. He's eating with a vengeance." I could hear the pride and satisfaction in her voice. She had suspected, weeks ago, something else besides a respiratory infection was plaguing our little one and had asked a friend of her father's, a well-respected doctor, to visit the DIF nursery and examine him. Ricardo, he'd pronounced, was gravely ill and needed immediate attention. He'd gotten our son an appointment, on that same day, with an endocrinologist buddy of his.

"The poor thing has a hole in his right eardrum," Ms. D said. "He'd been sleeping twelve to fourteen hours a day, on his right side, sucking on a milk bottle." He developed stomach reflux and suffered throughout the night when the acid spiked up his esophagus and erupted into his nose and ears, where it puddled and perforated the delicate tissue.

I listened. Gratitude replaced my annoyance. I thanked her for every tiny detail she attended to for the boys. Now, the government holidays were about to shut everything down for days, when the beastly sloth of a system would take almost as long to ramp up again. Nothing had progressed, there wasn't anything to cross off, notarize, or file away that brought us one step closer to our sons.

"I hope to have children of my own some day." Ms. D plunked down her words and paused until I wondered if we'd been disconnected. "They are special, these boys. You know that don't, you?"

"Yes." I could almost hear her armor crack. As I prepared to take the conversation one step further, she cleared her throat and stood up.

"Así es," she said.

CHAPTER XI

MARCH 1998

In early March we calculated that Marty and I had seen each other a total of twenty waking hours in February and spent much of that time wringing our hands over work, finances, the skyrocketing housing market, the adoption, the boys, and the sorry state of our lives. We had to have fun. We needed an adventure. But we were too tired and preoccupied to indulge and plan some fun. I think we had forgotten how.

A few days before St. Patrick's Day, the alarm rang and startled us awake in what seemed to be the middle of the night. Upset, because sleep was at a premium, I thought of three choice words, but held back when the reason came to mind: Marty was going to Sacramento. He was taking a stack of adoption documents to get certified with their apostil. A fancy name for a thick tri-circled raised seal only obtained in the capitol offices up north. We cut corners and tried to shorten the process whenever possible—we'd deliver the papers by hand during our upcoming visit with the boys.

"I'll make coffee while you jump in the shower." My mind was racing with the day's work schedule.

"Nah, go back to bed. It's way too early."

"We can go over the documents one more time," I suggested as I tied my robe while heading for the kitchen. A few minutes later I was in the steamy bathroom sitting on the toilet lid waiting for the coffee to brew.

"Do you think we'll ever have a normal life?"

"Normal? We're anything but normal, my dear."

"You know what I mean." I'd be forty-five at the end of the month and had always imagined myself a mother way before hitting this birthday. I'd officially be middle aged, barren and without children. A godforsaken biblical character shunned by her circle of women. I was foaming with melodrama and self-pity.

"Yes. Yes, we will."

I walked out of the balmy cocoon, came back with a mug of coffee, and decided to go back to bed. Uncertainty and fear plagued my thoughts until I had no choice but to plump up the pillows and sit up. Supposedly most pregnant women and mothers went through the same feelings at some point and yet nothing actually went wrong. I'd had these carbon copy, nagging thoughts about Sofia's birth mother, though, and my worst nightmare was confirmed. Going with your instincts was a funny, dicey matter.

We returned to DIF mid-March to good news. Ricardo's delayed birth certificate had arrived, so we could now begin the formal foster care and adoption process. Once in her tiny office, Ms. D opened up a hefty file of paperwork and receipts as she engaged in small talk and asked how we were doing. I settled in to the cold metal chair, allayed Ms. D seemed to be thawing out toward us.

"I have a request," she handed us a stack of medical receipts and bills. "I made copies for you. I wish I didn't have to ask, it makes me quite uncomfortable, but Ricardo's medical needs are—"

"We can't thank you enough," we interrupted. "We'd be glad to help in any way." I detected a tiny hint of gratitude, maybe tenderness, forming in one corner of her mouth. Then like a taut spring door, shut back to business.

Next we visited our social worker, who was impressed with the amount of requirements we had completed. Unfortunately one of the missing documents troubled her: the FM-3 visa. She suggested we contact a lawyer to help us procure one.

Ms. D accompanied us to an ultramodern firm downtown, the following afternoon, to meet with a Mexican lawyer who'd help us expedite the FM-3 visa, which allowed foreign citizens participation in Mexican business and transactions for a specific amount of time. The young man, in a tailored gray suit and manicured pianist hands, explained this took three months to process.

We groaned in unison.

A Barnum and Bailey type, the attorney seized upon our reaction and offered good news as well. He'd be going to México City within the next two weeks to conduct business with his corporate clients and would be honored to take the FM-3 visa applications on our behalf for a nominal fee. Hope seemed to warm up the air-conditioned conference room, but Marty was less optimistic. He diplomatically steered the lawyer into drawing a flow chart of the steps we still needed to get the boys home. He clarified each step as he crammed the elaborate process onto a legal-sized sheet of paper.

My stomach seized as the drawing illustrated our worst fears. We'd only scratched the surface of a glacier-sized process. Upon answering our questions, he recommended we obtain a FM-T, a typical tourist visa for six months, and that I renew my passport, upon returning to Santa Cruz, since it expired in August. That request sent a shockwave of disappointment throughout my body. August? As in the last month of summer?

He reassured me it was only a precaution. I chose to believe him. I was quite a pro at snatching up hope and perfuming myself in denial.

Afterward we took the boys to the hotel and while they played in the bath and turned into raisins, Marty and I sat on one of the double beds with our bulging portfolio, new applications, paperwork, post-its, and lists to plot and plan each hour we were in Juárez. When we'd finished or exhausted ourselves, we'd watch our sons' splash, giggle, and argue over toys.

Later we slathered them in baby lotion and took their mismatched clothes down to the laundry room and threw them away. I hesitated at the door and looked back at the garbage can, afraid that the clothes might follow me back to the room. Too bad there wasn't an incinerator.

The bitter cold kept us from the park, so we settled on a matinee of *The Borrowers* dubbed in Spanish.

"It's a great big screen, much bigger than the television in the older kids' classroom, where you see Barney the dinosaur," I promised. They clapped in excitement. They gasped at the ornate lobby and loved the tub of buttered popcorn and quart of soda we bought at the concession stand.

As we approached the double doors to the theater, Ricardo grabbed my neck in a chokehold. He buckled and whimpered.

Agustín thrashed, screaming, "The devil! The devil lives here," at the top of his lungs, heads turning towards us, as we entered the dim theater. Marty's calming words went unheard. We retreated to the lobby.

"Poor kid. What do we do?" Marty asked.

I told them we'd always keep them safe, that the devil didn't exist, and the dark wouldn't hurt them. It was only a color, like their T-shirts, not a thing or a monster. Ricardo chewed on his fist while Agustín seemed to size me up and consider whether to believe me. We promised we'd wait at the door, cracked open to reveal some light, until the movie started. If they didn't like the movie we'd leave. They whimpered and tugged at our sleeves when the lights dimmed, but as soon as the previews of a goofy remake of *Dr. Doolittle* came on, they laughed at the silly animals antics. They clapped and giggled throughout the movie, featuring tiny, mischievous people, and Ricardo fell asleep in my arms during the end. I was amazed at his spirit, how he made the most of everything regardless of his illnesses. I was pissed off, though, at whoever was responsible for terrorizing the boys with darkness and associating it with the devil. Was it someone at DIF, their birth mother, their first adopted parents?

CHAPTER XII

APRIL 1998

I awoke startled as if an earthquake had jolted the bedroom. The pitch black stunted my movement. I strained my eyes until a faint outline of my man, turned on his side, appeared. I pawed my way to the bathroom with clammy hands and a racing heart. An anxiety attack?

April 1st

> *Dream—I looked in the mirror and my face was sunburned, extremely red, puffy, burning, stinging and tight. I straightened my collar and it revealed a sunburned neck and chest as well.*

It hurt to touch. So what does sunburned mean? Perhaps being completely exposed to strangers who probe into every facet of our lives? Or was it being afraid of getting burned once again by the adoption process? I feel so vulnerable.

The week before Easter, we arrived greeting the staff by first names and no longer flinched at the pungent disinfectant. I scanned The Pit, but couldn't spot either one of them. Then I heard them. Above the fray and incessant noise of ninety-plus corralled children, I detected the caramel sound of their giggles, and my worries were tamped. The sound of *Mami*, *Papi*, urgent and excited, popping through the nursery, aimed in my direction, felt like the Fourth of July. The only thing better was feeling their little hands and legs wrapped around us, all four of us a pretzel of hugs and kisses. We no longer auditioned for the director or psychologist behind the two-way mirrors in the private family room before taking them for the weekend. The detours with our social worker petered out, our paperwork was up to date, but one constant remained. Ms. D appeared with a zippered, pinched expression as she motioned us into her office, apologetic upfront for delivering bad news. The increasingly complicated review cycle could take up to four more weeks with the upcoming holidays and unforeseen delays. My heart bottomed out.

By the time my Mother's Day flowers had wilted, I knew what I had to do. If my sons couldn't come to me, I'd go to them. Like Mohammed to the mountain.

"Are you sure?" Marty peered into my eyes. We'd spent the evening walking along the Santa Cruz wharf enjoying a breeze, without layers of clothing, when Marty stopped and took me by the shoulders.

"Yes. I can't go on visiting the boys and then leaving. We're going to screw them up if this goes on much more." I leaned against the railing, gazed out at the boardwalk lights in the distance, envying the families taking in the rides and cotton candy.

"Let's sleep on it. All right?" We strolled back and didn't exchange another word.

The following morning Marty suggested we call Ms. D and check in on the boys. She greeted us with an array of complaints. The boys were out of control and not obeying anyone because the staff was not their Mami and Papi.

"That's great, you know," I said after we'd hung up.

"That they're out of control?"

"Yes, it means they know we're the parents." I believed we had formed a bond. In my usual style, I'd only half thought out the money outlay—we were strapped—but I knew how inexpensively we'd lived in México before, plus we'd save money on last-minute airfares, hotels, rental cars, restaurants, etc.

Don't you see? I'd rationalize with Marty. It was the perfect transition for the boys and me, living in Juárez, same language, and culture in a regular home.

"Plus, I'll push the adoption process forward."

He'd debate and raise good points: our business and our relationship for starters. My colleagues and talented, energetic interns were completely ready to take Electric Mercado on, I countered.

"I could concentrate on work," he came around like a tanker, but continued playing devil's advocate.

"I'll be back in forty-five days."

"That's ridiculously optimistic," he warned.

We'd go back and forth for days, but he couldn't dissuade me. To Marty's credit and his enduring love, he threw up his hands, like Ronny Cammareri in *Moonstruck*, and did everything in his power to get me there. We were Team Santa Cruz. We'd go mid-June for Agustín's birthday. I had a month to prepare.

CHAPTER XIII

JUNE 1998

June 21ˢᵗ

Today, I become a mother. My arms will be full.

We crossed the bridge into México, like ants, in sweltering bumper-to-bumper traffic. Two boisterous, mariachi-singing kids jumped on the hood of our rental, sprayed our windshields, and wiped them clean before we could tell them a pair of clowns had already beaten them to it.

"Cleen, meester."

"Buen servicio."

They reached their hands into Marty's window, hawking more of their services as they eyed and counted their coins. As soon as we thanked them, but shook our heads, they tapped the car door and were gone. Heat waves formed in the distance. A wide swath of asphalt split into six lanes overloaded with vehicles and people as far as the eye could see. We moved a car length forward. Stopped. Minutes passed before Marty shifted out of park. Cars overheated. I fingered the car buttons then checked the glove box and console. Old ladies draped in dirty shawls begged hands upturned in supplication. Semi-trucks bellowed. Horns blew. Men hawked Jesus statues and velvet paintings of Elvis and mariachi crooner Vicente Fernandez. Buses spewed fumes. I smoothed out my skirt. Replayed everyone's good wishes. Pulled my hair back. Checked the bags under my eyes. All the while conjuring in glorious perfection what our Kodak moment would look like. Sappy and saccharine, but all mine.

I bought gum, feathery marionettes, ice-cold cans of anything, and kept my eye out for Carlos, a paraplegic who traversed from one side of Juárez to the other, on his over-sized, homemade board, somehow escaping reckless drivers, in freezing cold or hundred-plus degree weather. According to Rick, who had known him for years, the young man was a deaf mute and preferred the streets. Everyone looked out for him as he handed out thin, tiny slips of paper inked with prayers or affirmations and went out of his way to make eye contact, but never extended his hand. Never begged. Days were hellish and beastly, but the nights released the scum of the earth, the drug cartel thugs, and serial killers who slaughtered indiscriminately to send their enemies a message. Young girls disappeared in droves, but the city was too busy entertaining the noveau riche and greasing each other's palms to lift a hand.

"It's too bad Rick's not with us," I said. He'd been our rock through this, knew when to keep quiet, when to laugh, and, most important, when to pray.

We traversed through Juárez in one big messy lane heading toward DIF, past an office building that looked like a giant egg. It was a bright spot amid the blocks of empty junk and weed-filled lots. My favorite was the string of jewel-painted shops where the owners signaled the start of their day by washing down the sidewalk. The sound of bus traffic and the earthy smell of wet desert dirt and corn tortillas flooded my memory with perfect summer days at the home of my maternal grandmother, Nachu, in Nogales, Sonora. Now I'd create our own memories.

"We're finally here." Marty took my hand.

I clasped his hand. My throat constricted. My eyes stung. Could I really do this? On my own?

"I wish you would stay longer." That was the closest I came to confessing my fear.

"So do I, but Jannette will be here soon. That'll be a big help."

My younger sister, who, seven years earlier, had commandeered an emergency team during my ectopic pregnancy, was coming out from southern Arizona to help with the boys. I hung on to that.

My heart felt like a bag of cement one moment and light as meringue the next. Why was I so scared of what I most desperately wanted? Marty would commute every other weekend so that he could take care of our businesses and home. I looked over at my love and cohort, whose crimson, tired eyes looked hopeful as he stretched his arm out the window.

We arrived at DIF by 9:00 a.m. and were ushered into the director's office. Her eyes searched mine. We shook hands. She dropped her chin, trained her eyes on mine, and asked point blank, "Are you sure?"

Chin held high, I nodded. "My family will be visiting during the next month or so."

"Month?" The director questioned my length of time.

I capitulated to six maybe eight weeks. Tops.

She led us to an ordinary round office table where our provisional custody documents were laid out for us to sign. Would they turn watery, page by page, and dissolve like a desert mirage? I pinched myself. She left us alone to review the paperwork and within minutes Marty nudged me, pointing to a clause in the thick document that we couldn't take the boys out of the county, nor could I leave their side or Juárez until the adoption was final and the boys had their Mexican passports. I waved away his concern.

"Liz, what if it takes longer than forty-five days, or two or three months?

"No way. You heard what the lawyer said, that the FM-3 visa was the last big hurdle for us to jump."

"He also said we were going to have the boys home for Easter and then Mother's Day, remember?"

"True, but look at the list yourself. It's just a handful of items."

Marty looked up at the ceiling before speaking, "I'm sorry. I don't believe it's going to take forty-five days or two months. Look how long it's taken to get this far. You heard the director's opinion."

"I can't afford to think that way. It's my time here. I have to believe I can move things along and get us out of here as soon as possible."

"I know, but I don't want you to get resentful when it takes—"

"When?" I interrupted.

"All right, *if* it takes longer than you expect." We went back to the dense and convoluted paperwork.

"We're going to need a forklift to haul this paperwork around before we're done."

When I looked up twenty minutes later, I took the document and fanned myself. I stood up and loosened the dress away from my back and stretched out.

"Let's go get the boys, please."

He put up a finger, but his eyes never lifted from the table. Now, there was just one stack facedown waiting for the last two pages to complete the pile. Usually I would be as meticulous as Marty about reading any document, but today I wasn't signing a proposal or a contract. This was motherhood. I wanted my moment where I didn't have to wait for it any longer. I paced around the table on my tiptoes, cracking my knuckles and taking deep breaths as Marty flipped through the pages one last time.

The director returned, and within half an hour we had signed the papers. Tears blossomed in her eyes as we shook hands.

"Okay, let's go get our sons," Marty extended his hand to me. I felt jubilant and thought I understood what was on the other side of the nursery doors. I'd been an elementary teacher and an older sister to eight, I reasoned.

We were escorted to the nursery, where the feverish odor of too many children in close quarters seemed worse than in the buttoned-up winter months. Ancient, moaning water coolers blew stale, lukewarm air from one room to the other.

Marty leaned over, "This is the last time we'll be in here." He squeezed my hand. I bit the inside of my lip. My throat tightened. Could this really be happening?

Ms. D greeted us with her version of a smile, a lop-sided smirk, as she fanned herself with our file folder. We exchanged pleasantries and before starting my routine scan, our four-year-old jumped up on Marty.

"I told you I'd be back," Marty whispered to Agustín, who burrowed his face into Marty's shirt collar. The sight of bigheaded Ricardo waddling over refusing to be led by the hand completed my joy. I squatted and let him run into my body, where he nestled, and soaked my blouse with drool.

"Hola, Tesoro." I kissed his droopy cheeks. His head flopped back, a wide grin revealing a hodgepodge of teeth. I relished fitting him onto my hips and arm. Ricardo was playful despite ailing from reflux, an ear infection, a perforated right eardrum, and a skin condition, which sprouted blisters all over his tiny body. The visiting doctor, a charismatic and caring young man, prepared us with a sack of medicine, a detailed set of instructions, and future doctor appointments with two different specialists. He impressed upon us the importance of Ricardo's doctor's visits, carefully answered all of our questions, and then wished us the best of luck. The staff took turns coming by to congratulate us and tearfully kissed Agustín and Ricardo good-bye.

One of the nursery attendants grabbed my arm, looked deep into my eyes with a smile I'd seen on my grandmothers, and whispered into my ear in formal Spanish, "My dear lady, promise me, we won't ever see these two boys here again?"

I crossed my heart with my index finger.

She gathered me into her bosom.

"Hey Mami, let's go." Marty surrounded us with his free arm and joined up with the director and social worker, who led us through the facility like a parade. The boys waved, said good-bye a dozen times to everyone from the back of the nursery to the front lobby, and out we went through the front door and into the parking lot. We drove away to laughter and clapping in the back seat.

We'd immersed the boys in a bubble bath before noon and sprang into action. Marty left to buy a birthday cake while I unpacked a suitcase filled with party supplies. Agustín had turned four a week ago. I rearranged the furniture, decorated a table with bright paper plates, hats, and cups, and blew up an assortment of balloons until my cheeks hurt. The boys splashed, argued, and played peek-a-boo with me when I appeared at the bathroom door to check on them. When Marty returned with a melting chocolate cake, I finished decorating while he dried and dressed the boys. When they walked out of the bathroom they stopped, gasped, and stared at the transformation.

"¡Feliz cumpleaños, Agustín!" We congratulated our son, banking on the hope that he wouldn't know we were celebrating a week late.

Agustín clasped his little hands to his chest, jumping up and down at the sight of the balloons hanging from the lamp fixture and the streamers strewn around his birthday cake. We sang "Happy Birthday" while he grinned from ear to ear even though he didn't have a clue what the words meant. When it was time for Agustín to open his gifts, he asked, as we had expected, if there was one for his brother. There was. Ricardo sunk his teeth into it right away.

After their second piece of cake, Agustín asked, "When will Licalo get his party?" He still wasn't able to pronounce his R's. We explained they would each celebrate every birthday from now on. Agustín crawled up and slept on Marty's lap.

For the next two days, we headed out with marked-up newspaper rental ads, a city map, and drove around Juárez looking for a safe and convenient place to live. I looked forward to setting up our nest as I did in every place we ever traveled to, but we'd yet to come across an area that felt safe. The endless maze of asphalt, harsh concrete buildings, oppressive desert heat, and the number of dreadful apartments sent us back to our hotel room for a swim and nap.

Agustín continued to hide his toys behind the drapes. Marty commented on how easily he tired after just a few hours with the boys. I was grateful he brought it up first, because between the lack of sleep and the boys' constant activity I was burning a short fuse on both ends. I choked back tears when Marty told me he'd have to leave earlier than planned. There was another crisis at work. We'd gone to enormous lengths to keep our business afloat amid nightmarish obstacles. We were running on empty even though becoming a family buoyed us. After the fifth apartment door opened up to broken windows, scummy plumbing, and rooms overrun with insects, we bailed.

The Holiday Inn clerks took our map the following morning and circled the "safe" areas. The serial killer had been methodically raping, mutilating, and murdering young girls, and the police had not been able to apprehend him. They suggested we avoid any of the *maquiladoras* or the border areas where crime, they said, seemed to ooze from the ground up.

"Promise me you'll come back." I searched Marty's eyes. "As soon as possible."

I pushed down a wave of fear threatening to overwhelm me by listening to Agustín point out new objects to Ricardo, who acknowledged in his drooling gibberish. I had to think of the boys first. I swallowed my fears and helped Marty navigate through a neighborhood where we'd be safe.

Each neighborhood, or *colonia* to Mexicanos, had its corner store and concrete houses with the prerequisite wrought iron bars on all the windows and doors. The front yards were devoid of people until the evening, when the concrete steps were bearable to touch and the elderly sat outside, paper fan in hand, while the young ones chased a soccer ball underneath the streetlights.

After a dour morning of driving from one disappointing apartment to the next, we retreated to our favorite burrito place, where homemade flour tortillas were wrapped around a roasted and cheese-stuffed green chili dunked in crispy light batter and fried golden. No beans. No rice. No cabbage or lettuce nonsense. Juicy, delectable and all washed down with ice-cold sparkling limonada.

Afterward we approached Suites Victoria, turned to each other, and didn't drive away. The small bubble-gum pink complex, outlined in brilliant white, was in a nice neighborhood, down the block from a Catholic church, two blocks to a corner and stationary store, and a few blocks more to a good-sized park and soccer stadium.

Manuel, the supervisor, reviewed our application while I kept an even patter of white glove small talk.

"So you're from Sonora."

"Yes," I lied. My mother and all of her family were born and raised there, and some of them still lived there, except for my mother, who resided on the Arizona side.

He waved his portable phone at us to follow him out of the office past the set of concrete lions flanking the arched entrance. When the boys came face to face with the statues, their jaws hovered over their T-shirts, refusing to budge and pleaded to climb the lions. We picked them up and carted them off. Later, we promised.

"Most of the tenants are quiet, hard-working families and ambitious university students," he boasted and led us through the well-maintained complex and up a white metal staircase to a gleaming hallway draped in a purple bougain-villea. We'd seen a first-floor apartment that left us hopeful, but it faced a busy street.

"You're lucky we have two availabilities. We usually have a waiting list." He paused then flipped through the bulky key ring. The door opened to pleasing dark wood furniture. All of the plumbing in the bathroom and kitchen worked, and unlike the other apartments, there was no evidence of roaches or ants.

This two-bedroom apartment was on the second floor, where the kitchen and living room windows overlooked a row of tidy houses across the street, while the bedroom windows faced a sparkling blue pool and a tiny patch of scorched grass where the boys could play.

"Finally."

"Does that mean you want it?" Manuel asked. "We do have to paint and clean it first, so it won't be ready for another week."

We left a deposit, practically skipping back to the entrance, where we helped the boys scale the lions and hugged in relief, then headed to Sanborn's, an air-conditioned restaurant, to celebrate.

Our last two days together we spent stocking up on provisions and installing ourselves into a hotel with weekly rates. I clung to Marty, crying in the middle of the night while sirens wailed, traffic screeched, dogs howled, the sound seeming to ricochet into our bedroom window and intensify my desperation.

"It's threshold anxiety." Marty held me. "You do this before you go through a big change and then you're fine."

"This is different. I don't know if I can do this alone. In this city." I tried to explain but couldn't put into words the texture of my fear.

"Your sister will be here tomorrow and then I'll be back. And don't forget Rick."

Rick? Who was he kidding? There weren't enough hours in the day to attend to his parish in El Paso, family in Arizona, and his work with the Mexican orphanages, but Marty needed to know that I could do this without him. He was feeling incredibly scattered trying to push through two major events in our lives: adopting the boys and getting funding for the company. I winced when he said he felt like he was strapped to a speeding freight train headed for a concrete wall. I sucked it up. And like the little train that could, I pumped myself up with a fresh batch of future Kodak moments with the boys.

The next day Marty picked up my sister at the El Paso airport, dropped her off, and headed back to catch a flight home less than an hour later. I felt fortified by Jannette's presence and her easy way with the boys. She had Agustín and Ricardo in stitches as soon as she entered the hotel room and held them captive with her stories and photo albums she'd carted along. I loved her so much at that moment. She gave the boys a crash course on their grandmothers, their aunt and ten uncles, and their growing number of cousins.

Later that night when the boys had fallen asleep, Jannette and I had time to catch up.

"They're beautiful, Liz." She hugged me as we watched them sleep in one big tangle of arms and legs.

Ricardo woke up crying half a dozen times a night. I'd awaken with a dull headache, remembering how I'd had Sofia, our infant daughter, all to myself. I wanted the same with Ricardo, but Agustín woke up as well, worried and wanting to either join in or take over. I'd comfort them with my childhood lullabies while Ricardo lay on my chest and I cradled Agustín with my free arm. I envied my sister's ability to sleep through anything.

In the dim early morning I opened my eyes, groaning at my stiff neck and achy body, but relieved Ricardo was asleep. I would've paid a king's ransom for someone to take our little one from my arms, without waking him, or his brother, and place a steaming cup of coffee in my hands.

A couple of days later my frayed nerves unraveled when Agustín slapped my hands away as I changed Ricardo's diaper or washed his face and hands. Every morning he recited how he cooked for his baby brother, changed Ricardo's diaper, and fixed his bottle while his mother worked. I listened and understood where the little guy was coming from, but it was annoying. I explained I wanted to do all these things for both of them now, but welcomed his help.

He put his hands on his hips and said, "I'm the Papi. You help me. You're the baby."

When I chuckled, he screamed, "I'm the Papi," over and over. He didn't want to help. He wanted to be in charge of his brother as he had been. So at times, he was and other times Jannette and I distracted him while we changed Ricardo's clothes or gave him his medicine.

Not a day later, a misunderstanding between my sister and Agustín cracked the fragile gaiety of our newly formed family.

Jannette flew into our hotel room with Ricardo in her arms, "Agustín took off and I can't find him." I was folding clothes, savoring the size and fragrance of the boys' little T-shirts and socks.

My blood puddled around my ankles, but I grabbed my sister's extended hand and we ran faster than I can ever remember down one corridor and around another.

"I'm so sorry," Jannette said.

"It's okay," I lied.

My sister prayed to the Virgin Mary for help.

I stopped and described Agustín to every single person we came across.

"Don't worry, he's here somewhere."

"He'll show up. He's a kid."

On our way back to our hotel room we spotted Agustín. He hadn't run very far when he found an ideal hiding place: a huge potted banana plant. He peeked around the pot at the sound of my voice reassuring him that no one was going to hurt him, that no one was angry or upset with him. He stood up and with a bit more coaxing took my hand, but didn't want to go near Jannette. She was hurt and walked away.

Later as the boys napped, my sister came back. "This is just too difficult for me." Jannette wept.

"I need your help. I don't need you to fall apart." I was too tired to feel any sympathy. I couldn't console her.

The rest of the week my sister did help, but insisted on seeing the sights, and in the interest of keeping her happy and in Juárez, I pulled out a city map and pointed to the red stars that highlighted the points of interest: several new air-conditioned shopping malls, two museums, an ice-skating rink, a park, a soccer stadium, and an outdoor market. Jannette perked up and suggested the mercado would be a good place to start.

"The boys will love this," Jannette said as a handsome young waiter directed us to a table with a Corona Beer umbrella at one of the many outdoor restaurants surrounding the market. The water fountain entranced the boys, who stood in one spot, moving only to dip their fingers into the cool water, and daring the other to do the same. The waiter asked us for our drink order in English while he swayed to the MTV music and flirted with my sister, who lapped it up. In snooty curt Spanish, I informed him that we were from Sonora and squashed his turista routine.

"You didn't have to be so abrupt with him." She sounded wounded for both of them.

"I'm sorry, but I don't feel like I'm on vacation."

"Well, maybe that's your problem. Come on, loosen up."

"It's easy for you to do because you get to go home at the end of the week."

"Look, mariachis." She waved at them. The six-member group didn't need any more encouragement.

"Oh please, no." I love mariachis, but I don't like them playing at my table. My sister did and, like Nana Herminia, didn't hesitate to enthusiastically sing along.

"Just one song, I promise." Jannette stood up to greet them formally and requested her first of many songs. They were elated to serenade a true aficionado, and I couldn't turn them away, wearing heavy dark costumes in the scorching heat while they struggled to make a living. The boys came running over as soon as the music started and danced with Jannette, who showed them her favorite moves. I sat back and wondered what song Nana Herminia would request if she were with us and tried to pretend I was on vacation at least for this day.

CHAPTER XIV

JULY 1998

We began the blistering month at the bank in the usual long line of switchbacks that appeared to lengthen as we inched forward. What seemed like hours later, we reached one of four starched bank tellers who examined my driver's license front and back, tracing her manicured finger along the surface while shifting from one foot to the other.

"Please—wait—here. I'll—be—right—back." Her words thumped like a rubber stamp.

"They're traveler's checks." Jannette rolled her eyes and sighed, "Where's Karl Malden when you need him?"

After ten long minutes, Jannette nudged me. The bank teller walked toward us as if she were clutching a bouquet and heading to the altar. Step. Pause. Step. Pause. When she pushed my identification and traveler's checks back underneath the glass separating us, Jannette swore under her breath.

"You need the bank manager's authorization to cash these. You can wait over there."

Over there was a sprawling carpeted office area where spit-shined bank managers spoke in hushed tones to geisha-like secretaries. When the bank manager appeared at his desk, he rearranged his calendar, nameplate, and pens, then wiped lint from his suit. Meanwhile, we'd exhausted our bag of tricks and the boys seemed wired up to scale the walls or empty out desks, so I approached him. A gentleman, he stood up. I'm 5' 3" in flats. If we were standing side by side, his pompadour would just reach my shoulder. He pointed to the chair and grunted at me to sit down in front of his Cadillac-sized desk.

I presented my I.D. and checks before sitting down.

"Just leave the checks with me, come back tomorrow." He stood up.

I gripped my wallet and explained that on previous visits to this bank I'd been able to cash the checks right away.

A cynical smile replaced his officious manner. "Procedures have changed," he said and extended his hand to me.

"My son is ill and I need to purchase his medicine as well as other provisions."

"There isn't a person inside this bank without similar problems. Why should I treat you differently? Rules are rules." He pushed my I.D. and checks to the far end of his desk. My sister appeared like lightning, splayed her hands on his desk, and with a sickly sweet tone of voice asked him his name, rank, and serial number. This may have worked to my sister's advantage in the past, but today Napoleon reared up and told her it was none of her business.

"Your time is up," he said. When Jannette persisted, it only served to piss him off onto his tiptoes and beckon the bank guard.

"Wait outside. Now." I hissed into her ear.

A tottering old man sauntered over, tipped his faded hat at us, and patted the boys' cheeks, as I recalled my grandfather's doting hands cupping ours.

Jannette stepped back, scooped up the boys, and left with the bank guard shuffling behind her. I sat down and apologized. Poised at the edge of the chair, I begged him to cash just one check to tide me over until tomorrow. Miraculously, he did.

She meant well. As a little girl, she'd taken self-defense to heart and unlike me stood up to others regardless of size, weight, or age. As teenagers we'd run errands for our maternal grandmother who lived across the border. Once when a drop-dead gorgeous guy reached out, grabbed the end of my waist-length hair and wouldn't let go until I told him my name, my sister slammed the tip of her cowboy boot into his groin, pulled me away as he fell to his knees, and kept walking as if nothing had happened.

I never returned to that bank. I found out my ATM card worked in most newly installed bank machines. Mid-afternoons and nights, when the boys slept, Jannette filled those hours with art performance stories and a brand of humor our family honed to perfection. After our father died, we all but canonized my mother, and our goal was not to give her a reason to cry. Ever. My siblings and I took it a step further and choreographed Christmas variety shows, where every single one of us danced, sang, told jokes, played an instrument (one year, we added a ventriloquist act with Sammy, a Goodwill find), and performed skits to fill up the long hours till midnight when we opened our presents.

Days later my sister left. I hoped she'd convince others to visit. Now that I'd feasted on company, I felt lonelier than ever.

I also butted heads with a side of me I'd disowned. Losing control with the boys as my parents had with me. I'd never get angry with my kids. I'd never spank them. I'd be the best mom ever, just wait, and see. I'd show them. Once I left home and graduated with a Special Education degree, I'd figured sainthood was within reach. How could I not react to my kids' with Mary Poppins' cheer when Agustín ran off with strangers or they called out 'Mami, Mamee, Maameee, Maaameeee, Maaaameeeee' in the middle of the night just as a reprieve of silence had afforded me sleep? But it would take my entire being to keep the pressure-cooker anger six feet under and not cup my hand, arm extended back to swoop around, haul off, and give them one good whack. I'd arm-wrestle my anger, gasping as if winded, and keep my hands to myself, but I gave them scathing looks that chased them away. In a menacing silence I'd tower over Agustín, knowing I scared the shit out of him, and yet I'd advance until I only saw his pupils. My eardrums rattled with the thunder of my heartbeat. My rage seemed larger than myself. It recalled spankings on my backside, thighs, and shoulders from my mother and father. Something like the tug of a magnet lured me into the kitchen. I'd white knuckle the edge of the kitchen sink and slow my pounding heart. Was this how my mother and father felt? Was this normal? Was I having a nervous breakdown? Would this ever go away? When my anger was depleted, sadness crept out. I'd run to my sons and hold them close, apologizing and reassuring them it wasn't their fault. I was the mother.

July 10th

> *I was in the bathroom with the door closed when I heard them crying and calling my name. I can't go to the bathroom and close the door or they howl, so they sit inside the bathroom with me. Agustín wants to know why I have pubic hair and why I don't have a penis like them.*

Most early mornings we spent swimming, Agustín making great strides blowing bubbles and fetching brightly colored blocks underwater while Ricardo sat on an inflatable turtle on the first half-moon shaped step with his baseball cap pulled low around his frown. We had the pool all to ourselves when there was cool shade over most of the rectangular pool area thanks to the design of the apartment complex. At the deep end, propped on two opened clamshells, a voluptuous mermaid petted a dolphin. Agustín's curiosity prompted him to swim alongside me to the deep end. I scanned each apartment window and guessed what was going on inside as we cleaved the water. I heard mothers scolding, children answering, laughter, and meals being prepared. Treasuring the time to quiet my mind and distract me from obsessing over how long every upcoming requirement, step, or procedure would take.

By ten I chased them up the stairs while their laughter and happy shrieks echoed off the two-story high walls. By eleven we'd showered, ate a platter of fruit, and read until we all fell asleep. Like clock work, I'd wake up to find Ricardo sprawled on top of Agustín, deep asleep to the sound of the ancient evaporative cooler. Their dark feathery lashes twitched every so often. Inch by inch, I'd slide off the bed and sneak into my bedroom.

Sooner than expected, Ricardo woke me. I heard Agustín packing his little suitcase, again. My heart sank. He missed the people at DIF, where he'd spent thirteen months of his life. I recalled living with Nana Herminia, who lived right next door to us, and regardless of how happy I was to return to the mother ship after almost a year, I still missed my grandmother and her home. My son wanted to go back. We'd been warned that older children seldom made the transition; many would act out just to go back. Was this a sign? Shit. Now what?

I stood at the doorway, "Do you want us to go with you?"

He shook his head. Ricardo looked at his brother then at me several times before attaching himself to my knees.

"It's a long ways away, you know. Do you want me to make you a sandwich for the road?" Agustín nodded.

I went into the kitchen and made picadillo, a childhood comfort food, a savory meat dish spiked with chopped green olives. Agustín usually had seconds and thirds if there were any. I also made him a hefty sandwich and filled his canteen before Ricardo and I set the table for three. Agustín agreed he might as well have lunch with us; he'd have his sandwich later. He postponed his departure.

Some afternoons we'd eat lunch, tell stories, and afterward spread a blanket on the floor right under the water cooler vent to construct jigsaw puzzles and tell stories. A nap would follow and Agustín would forget about leaving. Other afternoons, he'd eat quickly and make a beeline for the suitcase and front door. I'd tell him that mothers always went halfway with their children when they left.

He'd nod. I'd grab an umbrella and my backpack and place Ricardo on my hip and off we'd go through the park to visit the fish and then have to stop for a Popsicle. By the time we'd head out again, after a toilet break, Agustín would say it was time for Ricardo's nap and we'd head back to Suites Victoria. He'd go tomorrow. We'd walk back sometimes in silence or with Agustín recounting life with his mom and dad. I listened to every word, hoping to help him soak up and hold on to the few memories he had.

I didn't dare tell Ms. D about Agustín wanting to go back, when we met at Ricardo's ear specialist a few days later.

"Being a mother suits you." Ms. D stopped me in my tracks as Agustín ran to her. Was he going to tell her? Ask her to take him back? My insides churned, but I suppressed puking all over her lightweight baby-blue suit.

I smiled and blinked back my emotions. If she only knew the undertow I was swimming against. I switched Ricardo to the opposite hip and wiped his drool before following Ms. D into the doctor's office.

"But you're losing weight. Are you all right?"

133

"It's the heat. I'm not used to it any more." I detected a slight drop in her shoulders and a release of clenched fingers as I answered her questions and joked. If she only knew what scraped against the back of my mind. If she only knew, I trembled. Maybe she was right when she voiced her protests? Perhaps this bright young social worker sensed something about me far beyond my citizenship. All I had to do was sit her down in the cool dim waiting room and come clean. Talk to her woman to woman. Bare my soul and unload my doubts and insecurity. What if she didn't pat my hand, tilt her head, and tell me I was being noble and shouldn't be too hard on myself? What if I rewarded her instinct, her gut? I'd fell any chance of becoming a mother. The boys risked going back to the orphanage.

The doctor playfully examined the boys while he congratulated me on how well Ricardo looked. Agustín was tall for his age and would grow like a string bean.

He pointed to Ms. D and said, "This young woman is, in large part, the reason your son is alive today."

Ms. D blushed. I thanked her. Agustín, sitting on her lap, planted a juicy kiss on her rouged cheek. The doctor, like a beloved uncle, asked her to take Agustín to the receptionist for a balloon while we talked. He plopped Ricardo into an examination chair, pulled down the magnifying lens, and had me peer into his ear. I winced at the sight of the hole in his right eardrum. When the doctor had said perforation, I thought tiny. Miniscule. This was a visible hole in his eardrum. He explained every detail of his diagnosis, treatment, and prognosis, and answered all of my questions. Yet, "near death" echoed in my mind the rest of the day.

After a longer than usual nap the boys climbed onto the sofa where I was completing a list in my journal. They were curious, pointing and asking about my writing, sketches, and calendar. I opened to a blank pair of pages and placed Agustín's palm on one side then traced his long delicate hand, before doing the same for Ricardo on the page opposite. They clapped in awe. It was magic. I helped them write their names. From then on they gathered flowers and leaves for me that we scotch taped on pages, where they doodled and drooled.

A few days later we ventured into Futurama, a gigantic grocery store where I placed both boys in one of the doublewide grocery carts and off we went shopping. Agustín organized every item I gave him into the cart; he stacked the single-serving yogurts in one corner and cheese in the other. I promised he'd have a yogurt as soon as we got home. A few minutes later, Ricardo held onto a bag of limes while his older brother hoisted a watermelon into the cart then grabbed a yogurt and pulled at the lid.

"Not yet." I explained we needed a spoon, but he wouldn't let go of it and promised to just hold it.

Before heading to the cash register, I stopped at the bakery, but kept one eye on the boys as I made my selection. When I turned to put the bag in the cart Agustín was feeding Ricardo handfuls of yogurt, which was dripping onto the floor. I saw matador red. I pried the container from his death grip. His nails-on-a-chalkboard shrieks culminated in him peeing all over the cart, food, and floor. My heart pounded. My mouth went dry. Ricardo howled while yogurt ran down his shirt. A battalion of eyes and dirty looks followed us as I searched for a garbage can, an employee, and a way out of this mess. Two sympathetic employees arrived with towels and a mop, and after we wiped Ricardo down, suggested I wheel the boys out in the cart. I nodded. I apologized and choked on my embarrassment.

Once outside I scooped Ricardo out of the cart, but Agustín wouldn't budge. I growled and yanked my oldest onto the sidewalk. Folks outside Futurama stared at our encore performance of madwoman with screaming children. Cruella de Ville came to mind. I hailed a taxi, but the driver pretended not to see me and sped by. We took the bus home and I got off a stop early after other riders complained when Agustín threw himself on the floor and finished peeing. An older gentleman helped me get him off the bus and assured me his kicking and punching hadn't hurt at all.

I was incapable of chronicling my anger and my close calls. Much less the times I did spank them. Instead, I knelt as if to pray and retched, my hair pulled back while tears mixed with snot plunked into the toilet bowl. I wasn't mother material. It didn't quite match up, how I felt, and other mothers' looked and acted. I just didn't stack up. Is that why fatigued Mexican mothers looked at me sideways, as if saying, what in the hell were you expecting? One too many Kodak commercials for you, gringa. Snap out of it! They're healthy, good natured, and good looking to boot. Count your blessings and shut the fuck up.

I'd cower at the thought of admitting failure and instead channeled Scarlet O'Hara's tomorrow is another day. I'd tamp down my guilt and smother their day with play, fresh fruit paletas, and adventure.

After a shower, I put Agustín down for a nap. He cried off and on for hours even though I held him, offered snacks, played music, told him a story. I left their bedroom with an overwhelming urge to muzzle his crying with my hand. I lay awake that night in a spiral of regret. Why had I been so against fertility treatments? I missed Sofia. I made a mental list of all the wonderful things I loved about the boys. I replayed lovely family scenes, but I couldn't subdue the feelings. Maybe, like thunderclouds, they'd pass?

Mid-July marked the beginning of the desert valley's monsoon season, which announced its arrival with a fireworks display of sky-to-sky lightning and flooding rains. The boys screamed and raced over to me when lightning cracked right outside the front door. Ricardo clung to my neck and Agustín had seemed to fuse himself with my hip and thigh. I took in the soft fragrance of their skin, loved how their warm breath tickled the hollow of my shoulders. I held them both, together whenever they wanted.

As I closed curtains and doors, I remembered Herlinda, our housekeeper, doing the same thing when we were home alone with her. I stopped short at covering the mirrors, blessing the boys with holy water, and stashing them under the dining room table. But we lay on a blanket on the dining room floor, away from all of the windows, and I told them that the angels were playing ball up in the clouds. Their expressions changed. Was it really that easy? Agustín almost smiled and reassured his little brother. Ricardo stopped gnawing on a corner of *Goodnight Moon*. I turned on the swamp cooler, hoping the raspy sound of the motor would drown out the thunder. But the inevitable happened— a booming bolt of lightning shook the windows and lit up the living room. Agustín and Ricardo yelped, jumping into my arms and shaking with fear. They stayed attached to me the rest of the day.

When I had to go to the bathroom they came along as usual. I closed the door behind us and they played contentedly. I realized the bathroom was the quietest room since it lacked a window and was flanked by adjoining rooms. We collected our things and hunkered down there until the storm passed hours later. From then on, as soon as we heard the raindrops pelting the roof and windows, we grabbed toys, blankets, and books and holed up in our bunker, the bathroom.

I'd drawn a July calendar on the back of my journal and crossed out each day upon waking as I drank coffee and made a list of things to do. A pang for my old life, my office, the camaraderie, and hustle at work overcame me. Not at all what I had anticipated. I daydreamed, wondering what my colleagues were up to, envying them. I'd pontificated I was ready for a break and wouldn't miss any of the Internet rat race. But I did. I missed it all and longed more than anything else to have a phone in the apartment to call out and receive support and reassurance from family and friends. If only I could curl up at night after the boys went to sleep and talk to Marty like we used to when we both traveled. I would vent, ask for advice, and find out what I was missing back home. But that luxury was out of my reach. We weren't Mexican citizens with established credit and hadn't signed a yearlong lease on the apartment. The public telephone next to the pool would have to do.

"Any news from Ms. D?"

"The adoption notice will be in the newspapers and we're waiting on the petition. Again." Monotone was the best I could muster.

"Do you have any hankerings? What can I bring down for you?"

A substitute, I thought. Bring someone down here to take my place for a week. A placeholder. No one would know. One week. I salivated at the thought of sleeping in my own bed, having my life back for a bit before taking up the cause again.

The sharp phone beep signaling my phone card was out of time forced a hasty good-bye.

To console myself, we'd head to the air-conditioned mall, pick up a packet of photos, and lounge by the cool indoor water fountain with a huge bag of salty popcorn to see what we'd done the week before. The boys giggled and covered their eyes at seeing themselves frolicking in the apartment pool, walking to the corner store or park, brushing their teeth, cooking, or taking a bath.

I augmented the photos in the album with postcards of Juárez, along with Mexican paper money and coins, their little drawings, and even the receipts from the hotel, Sanborn's, and the mall. The boys needed tangible proof of their history. On my thirtieth birthday my mother had given me my baby book filled with my elementary report cards, sloppy drawings of turkeys and Easter bunnies, homesick letters I'd written while away on a summer vacation, and gawky school pictures. I treasured every bit of me that my mother kept and returned.

By the third week of July, the boys seemed to thrive with a routine, and I was glad to have activities that helped make the blistering days go by faster. Ricardo woke up like a wind-up toy with one mission: Find Mami. We'd cuddle. We'd play. He was such a baby. I relished this most tender of moments then felt bittersweet for my oldest. When Agustín joined us, he'd scoot Ricardo away to have me all to himself. When I played music and danced with Ricardo in my arms I'd do the same with Agustín. I became acutely aware of my time, actions, and affections with each of them and made sure they both received the same amount of attention. If I pitched a ball one time less or skipped a twirl in a dance step, Agustín would let me know. Was this how it was with twins, I wondered? My back, hips, and arms ached at night from carrying my little boys off and on all day, but I didn't have the heart to refuse Agustín, who was mimicking Ricardo's baby talk, crawling around instead of walking, and wanting to wear a diaper. Luckily they wanted to do everything I did, so I had them help me make the beds every morning, set and clear the table, fold laundry, collect the trash, put groceries away, and pick up their toys.

I went out of my way to tell my oldest how great he was at helping and how lucky I was to have an older son to help me.

"Do I help you more than Licalo?" He needed constant reassurance. It reminded me of growing up with ten siblings—we auditioned every single day for prettiest, smartest, and funniest. The competition was stiff, my siblings were born photogenic, and witty, which was one of my mother's weaknesses.

Ricardo on the other hand was oblivious and preoccupied with stuffing whatever he found on the floor into his mouth. One muggy afternoon he scaled the sofa and launched himself backward, missed the cushions, and crash-landed on the floor.

The loud thwack like a watermelon cracked open got my attention, but the ear-splitting shrieks curdled my blood. I found him writhing on the floor with a goose egg of a bump. I carried him over to the freezer with Agustín hanging on to my shirt, and pulled out an ice tray, dumped the cubes on the counter, wrapped a couple in a dishtowel, and gently placed them on the back of his head. Ricardo thrashed and kicked while trying to snatch the ice cubes off his head. Agustín thought I was hurting Ricardo and came to the rescue by pummeling me. I was surprised at how hard they could both hit. I was afraid to loose my grip on Ricardo and didn't have a free hand to calm Agustín so I snarled from a recess tucked deep inside me that rumbled and ended in a hiss: "Stop it." Their little hands froze, suspended in mid-air. They burst into tears. They sobbed even more as I tried to explain myself to a couple of toddlers. I gave up and sat on the kitchen floor ready to burst into tears myself.

As the last week of July counted down, I dispensed with naps, forgoing the much-needed sleep because of Ricardo's new game. I awoke one too many times, groggy and disoriented, to find Agustín fast asleep, minus Ricardo. I'd hear the toilet flush and flush and flush again. I'd leap out of bed in one fell swoop and reach the bathroom to find the toilet bowl overflowing while Ricardo splashed his feet in it. He had a shit-eating grin right out of *Animal House*. I saw John Belushi drooling down the front of his T-shirt, pumping one fist in the air, ready to pull the handle with the other. I grabbed him while a horseshoe-shaped curtain of water and globs of toilet paper flowed over the bowl. He wrestled out of my arms and threw himself on the floor, bellowing, kicking, and splashing water everywhere. Agustín appeared at Ricardo's side, but his little brother pushed him away. While he threw his tantrum, I inspected the toilet. Ricardo had stuffed a half dozen or so fist-sized, plastic geometric shapes down the toilet before securing it all in place with a roll of toilet paper. I was tuckered out and in no mood to clean up the slushy mess. I scooped up and held him as he whimpered and shuddered into a long drawn-out yawn.

Frowning, I pointed at the toilet bowl, shook my head, and said, "No."

Agustín reared up and warned his little brother to behave or he would no longer be my son.

I froze. Where had he heard that? The toilet now seemed a minor annoyance. I knelt down and tucked them in close.

"We're a family forever, mijitos. It doesn't matter what you do or how angry Papi or I get. We love you. You'll always be our sons."

On one of our many early evening neighborhood walks, we discovered a larger, well-stocked corner store. I marveled at aisle upon aisle of assorted selections of groceries. I took my time browsing and let the boys examine the cans of vegetables, sponges, and boxes of cereal as we made our way up and down each aisle, picking only those few items I could fit into my backpack. While deciding between a can of Serrano or Chipotle chiles an explosion of lightning made the store lights flicker. The boys yelped, grabbed the sides of my dress, and started wailing. A series of thunderclaps made them screech louder.

I tucked a few more items into the backpack, grabbed the boys, and headed for the checkout line. There were at least three and four people lined up at each cash register. I was counting on the next deafening crack of lightning to alleviate the long lines, but no one stepped away. Everyone had dinner to prepare. Rain pelted the storefront windows as customers and employees remarked that it would pass as fast as it had come. I walked the boys over to the Popsicle icebox, careful to avoid scanning the stack of daily newspapers with gruesome headlines of incessant violence in Juárez. As I pointed to different Popsicles, I noticed water rising to the top of the tall curbs. The streets were already flooded. How would we get home? We had always been inside during one of these rainstorms. The lightning had moved on and we could only hear it faintly in the distance, but the rain wasn't letting up. As Ricardo's Popsicle dripped down his arms and legs, the rain slowed down to a drizzle, and the store manager, who was smoking a cigarette by the front door, suggested we make our way back to Suites Victoria now instead of later. Calling a taxicab was out of the question, he said, everyone avoided the area during flash floods. I thanked him, put the backpack on, picked up Ricardo, saddled him onto my hip, and told him to hold on tight.

With Agustín's hand firmly in my mine, I told them we were going on an adventure where we'd surely get wet. Their curious smiles bolstered me. I counted to three and we stepped off the curb into the knee-high water and laboriously crossed the street while I tried to maintain my balance. Once back up on the sidewalk we retraced our steps back home as fast as Agustín could keep up with me. We reached the end of the block. I adjusted my backpack and switched Ricardo to my other hip. You are so brave, I cooed at them. Maintaining a Vanna White smile, my oldest saw right through it and clamped down on my hand until it went numb. I sang "El Rancho Grande," one of Nana Herminia's Sunday afternoon songs with a happy-go-lucky melody about a young man boasting of a young gal wooing him back to the ranch with a pair of wool and leather underwear. Go figure. Then Agustín, not to be outdone, was in the middle of his duck song when an alluvial wave drenched us to the bone in a matter of seconds. I pulled Ricardo and Agustín's baseball caps forward to keep the rain from their eyes and laughed, pretending the heavy rain was fun, but the boys didn't join in. I was counting my blessings, when a spider web of lightning seemed to parachute down on us. They shrieked. The thunder boomed. They clawed at my clothes. It seemed Ricardo wanted to crawl inside my dress. The roar reverberated all around us.

"Mami." Agustín tensed and yelled, "Accidente."

I told him not to worry. I had almost had an accident myself.

We had to get cover immediately. I scoured both sides of the streets for an awning, a porch, or a garage with its door open and kept walking. Safety was four more blocks away. Up ahead a narrow overhang came into view. I took long, deliberate steps toward it. Halfway to it, a lightning bolt hit so close, we sank into a huddle. I closed my eyes. The acrid smell punched through our nostrils. The boys felt limp.

It seemed an hour had gone by before we finally opened the front door to our apartment and plopped down on the floor sopping wet and exhausted. Agustín made me promise we'd never go on another adventure ever again.

Marty arrived a couple of hours later to open arms, a feast, and stories about our new home, neighbors, and our adventure. I relaxed and savored the few days we had with the boys and each other. We did the same things, but it felt different. We ate the same things, but they tasted better. The boys cried less at night. I slept more. Marty napped with the boys while I went out alone. I had company, help, and someone to hold me when I cried or felt overwhelmed. His visits, though, only added up to two or three days at the most.

Early Monday morning before Marty left back to Santa Cruz, we went to the passport office and got in the short Information Only line and were back out the door in under an hour after receiving the best news to date.

"Did I hear her correctly?" I asked as we headed toward the car.

"Yep, you did."

"It's going to take one day to get the boys passports?"

"As long as we arrive by seven in the morning with three copies of everything they've asked for." Marty fished for the rental car keys with his free hand as he adjusted Agustín on his hip.

I clutched his hand, feeling a surge of hope. This meant we would be heading home by early-to-mid August at the latest. He flashed me a wide grin and I settled back into the car seat and felt that I could do this. I could live here for another few weeks. Everything would change for the better once we got home.

July 26th

Couldn't sleep most of the night. I made the mistake of watching the nightly news while I was stretching my aching body. The newsman gave a chilling update on the serial murderer and emphasized that he preyed on young women walking to and from las maquiladoras. I've been haunted by thoughts of why the boys' birthmother didn't return to DIF. What if she had planned on returning, but had been a victim of the serial murderer? I felt an icy, nauseous jolt. She had worked at the manufacturing plants.

A few days later the three of us arrived at Registro Civil by 8:00 a.m. to request original birth certificates for the boys. Ms. D reminded me we would be lucky to have all the documents ready and the judge's approval by the end of August. I had only two more days of July to cross off and many more hurdles to jump. The punishing heat was over one hundred ten degrees by noon every day. We joined a long line forming outside the building. We filed in upstairs a few feet at a time. By ten o'clock we settled at the top of the stairs outside the double doors. By eleven we passed people in line for the cashier at a snail's pace. There was no ventilation in this room. The boys were lethargic. We finally got to the lobby—there were chairs. Ricardo fidgeted and perspiration dampened his shirt. I felt stupid for not packing water. I found some hard candy in the backpack.

When we got to the receptionist, she instructed me to pay for the birth certificates first. I needed a receipt. I was livid at her nonchalance, but only groaned at her and got in another fucking line. At half past noon, I was halfway to a cashier. Ricardo was asleep in my numb arms, drooling on my left shoulder. Agustín dozed against my legs. I had, of course, chosen the slowest line inside the suffocating room, packed so tight with people their breath landed on my bare shoulders. When I got to the head of the line, I sat Ricardo on the counter to forage in the backpack for my wallet. The cashier pinned her eyes on mine and with a sideways jerk of her head told me to move Ricardo.

"Just a moment, I'm pulling out my wallet."

"Sorry, but I get in trouble when the counters break, so move him." She had the receipt pad with a set of rubber stamps I needed, so I resisted the urge to slam the money on the counter. It was past two o'clock when we got back home with nothing more than another receipt to return on the thirty-first for the birth certificates.

As I hunted through the four fuzzy channels on the clunky black-and-white TV, the evening news was on most of them, warning of marauding gypsies sighted around Juárez trying to con their way into peoples' homes. The neighbors, Manuel, and even Ms. D reminded me of their tactics: a child knocked on the door asking for help. Once the door was opened, the rest of the gypsies swarmed the house, overtook the family, and like vultures stripped the household of food, money, and valuables. Great! I puzzled the furniture against the front door and left a bucket on the very edge of the coffee table, so a slight movement of the door would upset it and alert me. I hoped. Stress dreams were no longer about botched-up work projects or missed deadlines.

I woke up with a nasty cold, but swam with the boys and took them on a long walk. I needed the routine even more than they did. It kept me from thinking too much. After the walk, I laid down, the boys playing on the floor next to me. I turned on the TV and Oprah's summer reruns were on. This episode highlighted the challenges of being a parent. Every word from a frustrated parent was like a salve. Every time an expert or Oprah said that being a parent was the hardest job on earth, I nodded and cried in gratitude.

Later, I called my mother-in-law in New Jersey. She listened while I went on for a good twenty minutes. Then we swapped child-rearing stories and for the first time I heard that my frustration and anger toward the boys was common. My mother-in-law now insisted I call her collect, anytime day or night.

"It's the least I can do, when you're in that hellhole with my grandchildren, and I'm in the comfort of my home." She had been following the news about the crime and violence festering in the city. I'd expected my mother on the other end of the line, comforting me in Spanish, but my seemingly brusque mother-in-law was the one to toss me a lifeline.

Much later that night I heard noises outside our front door. My hand shot underneath the pillow for the mace. My eyes went to the bedroom door. I tiptoed to the living room. Someone or something scampered back and forth. Terrified, I backed up against the wall. Serial killer, gypsies, rats? My eyes adjusted to the dark and finally rested on the bucket. I slumped to the floor, hugged my knees, and tapped my heels together. I just wanted to go home. I muzzled my sobbing afraid I might miss something. I stayed up listening to every sound while my heart jerked around in my chest.

On the last day of July we joined the early birds, forming a line inside the Registro Civil to pick up the boys' birth certificates. A statuesque woman came over to me while I read to the boys. She discreetly asked me if I was adopting the boys. I nodded. She caressed the boys' heads and faces. Said she had seen us in here last week and was impressed by how well behaved the boys were. I thanked her and couldn't help but feel suspicious of her actions. She pressed her business card into the palm of my hand and told me she worked in the back offices after I cautiously answered more of her questions about our adoption process. "You are doing a beautiful and selfless act of kindness. You have found a friend here at el Registro for life." She took my hands in hers and said I was to ask for her anytime I had business here. I left feeling ashamed for doubting her genuine act of kindness.

CHAPTER XV

AUGUST 1998

I jabbed at the paper, sketching an August calendar on the back of my journal. Why hadn't I been courteous and just taken one from the toothy-grinned owner when we entered his cluttered store to buy drawing supplies, notebooks, or just delight in the gigantic piñatas hanging from the ceiling and lining the walls? Because everything seemed to matter, was a sign, a symbol, and reason to go on with the plan. A calendar would certainly jinx the adoption process and extend the upcoming deadlines from days into weeks. Hanging a calendar was somewhat akin to putting down roots for me. It meant that I was all right with settling in to this apartment. Next I'd have plants and a throw rug.

For the same reason, the only clock in the apartment was a small traveler's version in my bedroom. I didn't need to be assaulted by the languid movement of the clock's hands. It seemed that the mounting heat was slowing down the earth's rotation and melting away any progress towards the end of each day. Yet at the same time, I wanted the minutes to stretch out so that our paperwork was able to travel from one desk to another, collect another round of rubber stamps, and reach the hands of a judge pleased with its contents and poised to sign his approval and pass it on to the next judge before the end of a day.

When neighbors greeted us, I covered up my sour mood with a flimsy veneer of good cheer. I kept myself in check when anyone inquired how the adoption was coming along. Agustín listened to every word I said and later in the day would parrot back entire exchanges I'd had with a neighbor or Manuel the supervisor. Sometimes it brought me to laughter, other times, it felt creepy. Was this normal? I'd ask my mother when I called her for her birthday on the seventh.

The heat pitched, reaching one hundred nineteen degrees by eleven in the morning and hovering there until six o'clock or so when it stubbornly began to drop a degree until settling at ninety-five. We took advantage of the evening breeze after dinner and strolled around the deep-pink complex, greeting neighbors and listening to the cornucopia of sounds emanating from the cinder block building. The boys chased after flying beetles that thwacked against the tiles and were on the lookout for the skinny cat with the chopped-off tail. When we reached the far end of the second floor, we climbed the concrete staircase and sat on the warm top step. I spoke with both of the boys about being a family.

As Agustín and Ricardo inched closer to me, I recounted how much Marty and I wanted to have a family and that one evening we had gone for a walk on the beach. As the sun was setting toward the ocean, the moon was rising, and we saw one little face smiling down at us from the sun and another from the moon. The very next morning Uncle Rick had called us and told us that there were two little boys who wanted a Mami and Papi. So we got on a plane and came to Ciudad Juárez, where we met them.

"Was I the sun or moon?" Agustín asked.

Without hesitation I answered that I saw his face on the moon and Ricardo's on the sun. Agustín bolted and ran to the balcony, where he pointed to a translucent new moon, as a melting buttery sun receded behind us.

"The moon is mine, Licalo. The sun is yours."

The boys played on their bedroom floor with toys after their nap the next day, and I retreated to my daily refuge, Oprah. Watching the shows, I added to my careful notes: appropriate discipline techniques, natural consequences work best, and the importance of apologizing to children when we hurt them in any way. This was a revelation to me. Apologizing to children? In my family, children apologized, period. Parents equaled being right one hundred percent of the time. Children were seen and not heard unless adults demanded a performance of some insipid school or recital trick. It didn't matter whether the spanking, ear pulling, or pinch on the upper arm was justified. It didn't matter if they left welts or broke through skin. Heaven help us if we cried or were brash enough to defend our actions. A vein would protrude over my mother's arched eyebrows; her green eyes darkening like old moss if we questioned her authority. This was her house, her rules. When we ran for our lives to avoid a spanking, my mother chased us, equally fast on high heels or in fuzzy magenta slippers. If my mother couldn't catch us and we were too dumb not to let her, she used whatever she had in her hand to show us who was boss. My mother possessed a powerful right-handed throw and could land a russet potato right between our shoulder blades from the kitchen to the front door, a good eighty feet away. The sound of her satisfied laughter, as she felled you, flat on your face and gasping for air, only added insult to injury.

Not me. No siree. I'd show the mother of all mothers I could be different, possibly better.

What began as my escape with my hour of Oprah became my classroom time. I laughed out loud when an expert stressed the importance of finding time to be alone and teaching kids to respect mommy's time. A closed door between us still frightened the boys, so for the time being, early morning and late at night was my only refuge. I'd never given a thought to any of these things before, because I was dead set that not much was going to change. I could juggle it all. I *was* every woman, like in Oprah's theme song. My family and friends warned me, but I, in total ram fashion, disregarded their advice. What a stubborn fool I'd been. Now, I got it! What my co-workers and friends had been trying to get me to stop and see was now crystal clear. I was discombobulated by the ferocity of the change in our lives and hadn't anticipated this fever pitch of loneliness. Life would improve once we got home became my mantra. I repeated it while we walked, swam, when I showered, fell asleep, cooked, even when I read to the boys. Peace of mind was right over there, on the other side of the border fence.

By the end of the first week in August, I hadn't heard from Ms. D, so I called her. The receptionist always dispatched a couple of people to find her and made sure I wasn't kept waiting long. She knew I was at a pay phone and would put other calls on hold to take care of mine.

Ms. D came on, sounding out of breath as she asked me if I had a pen and paper ready. Glad we were dispensing with the uncomfortable small talk, I wrote down the name of the magistrate who was overseeing our adoption petition. Finally, we were rolling along in an official process with an end in sight. We were weeks away from heading home.

She answered my questions, and then said she had more information for me. My pen was poised. Marty would be delighted—good news for a change. We would skip the morning swim and go to Sanborn's air-conditioned restaurant and department store instead to celebrate.

Ms. D had met with the magistrate who oversaw that the petition was complete and correct before arriving at the judge's chambers. When I tilted my head to cradle the receiver I spied my eldest. I dropped the phone receiver and dashed after Agustín who was peering, on tiptoes, into a neighbor's window. I grabbed him and gave the boys a piece of chewing gum and promised more if they stayed at my feet. I picked up the phone and, without explaining, asked Ms. D to please continue. I furiously scribbled down words and phrases, smudging the page with my left hand.

When Ms. D concluded, I repeated the information back to her. When it dawned on me that once the judge in Juárez reviewed and approved the petition, he'd send it on to a judge in Chihuahua City, who'd send it on to a judge in México City, who'd send it back to Juárez before granting the final adoption, I turned away from the boys and moaned into the wall. Ms. D confirmed this process would take another six to seven weeks, *if* our petition was in order and the three judges were amenable to an American couple adopting Mexican children. She reiterated the magistrate's gloomy fact that México had approved less than a handful of adoptions to American parents in the last five years. I squeezed the phone receiver with both hands, imagining the feel of her neck, and before I swore at her like a gutter drunk, I hung up.

I dialed Marty's phone number, doubled over with the weight of what this new information meant.

"You were right," I wailed. "We'll be lucky if we get home by the end of September."

Marty groaned.

"I don't know if I can do this, Marty." My body shook as I wept, then in mid-sentence I felt Ricardo lifting himself up on my legs. I turned to find Agustín clutching his hands, his eyebrows knit together while Ricardo patted my left knee. I snapped out of it and regained enough composure to smile and reassure them. I had Marty talk to Agustín while I held Ricardo, who looked deep into my eyes and then placed his head on my shoulder and patted my back. Now it was Marty's turn to write as I listed the details. He'd call the director and confirm the information just in case Ms. D might have gotten confused. We were hopeful the fourth review was redundant and a mistake on Ms. D's part.

"Remember, this will be over. Don't lose hope. I know how difficult this is for you, but it will be over soon. I promise."

"Meanwhile I can just pretend there isn't a serial killer that's murdered over eighty women roaming the streets. I can also just ignore the drive-by shootings, the bands of gypsies, and pretend it's normal to barricade the front door every night. Now I'm told I have at least another six weeks in this hellhole and you don't want me to lose hope. Well, I have news for you, Mr. Picco, there is no hope in Juárez! You have to give me more than hope." I spat out my desperation.

"I'll move my schedule around. I'll be there on Thursday for a long weekend— that's only five more days. Call my mother. You need to let it out."

"I need to get out of here," I growled. "I can't believe how stupid and naïve I was." I was grateful the boys didn't understand English yet. It afforded me some privacy from Agustín's endless questions.

After I hung up, I blew my nose, peeled a couple of oranges for the boys, and watched them happily suck on each section while the juice burst from their mouth. I looked over my notes. We wouldn't be home for Marty's birthday. We would be here for another miserable season.

I dialed my mother-in-law's number, waiting for the familiar international dial tone when my hair was yanked backward until I winced in pain. I spun around, ready to fight back, when I smacked into a pair of Dolly Parton boobs spilling out of a gold lamé bathrobe. The shellacked face snarled from above, eyes concealed by gaudy gold-framed sunglasses and garnished with brassy orange tousled hair. The Baja Barbie look-alike had Agustín in a death grip by the scruff of his neck. I snatched him from her. My hands tucked them both behind my rigid body.

"Motherfucking kid, won't let me sleep!" She pointed at her window where my oldest had been bouncing a ball. She threatened to complain to the manager and said that next time she would take matters into her own hands if I couldn't control the creatures. In an instant, I was back in the sixties behind the junior high school gym where Germ, who sported a Kewpie doll face and a mean right punch, was bullying me. I knew from experience to shut up and wait for a pause in her tirade to apologize. She had no intention of letting me utter a word as her crescendo of profanities opened doors and windows around the complex. Satisfied with a generous audience and my cowardice, the woman pivoted, military style, muttering under her breath that some people worked for a living as her high-heeled sandals clicked on the walkway and her robe undulated behind her ala Darth Vader.

Part of me wanted to chase after her, jab my finger into her silicone-injected chest, and threaten the vulgar bitch that next time she touched my kid, I'd gouge her eyes out. The other part knew it would be ugly for the boys to watch her pummel me. I grabbed the boys and high-tailed it back to the apartment like skinny, twelve-year-old Liz Raptis haunted by jeers and embarrassing laughter. When Agustín asked me who that lady was, I looked him square in the eye and said that wasn't a lady, but a fire-breathing dragon who hated kids.

Once the sun weakened in the early evening, we went for a swim out of desperation to distract my brain from the conversation with Ms. D, the new timeline, and all the things that could possibly go wrong.

Manuel, the supervisor, tinkered with the pool filter at the deep end. The boys ran over to say hello, squatting next to him as he worked. The water seemed an artificial blue. The chlorine kicked my face, but I closed my eyes and treaded water, listening to Manuel answer each of their questions as if they were his apprentices. When he was done, the boys helped put away the tools and joined me in the shallow end to show off their underwater skills. I asked about his family. He puffed up, tucked in his shirt with one swoop of his hand, and said they'd be at the festival in the park later tonight. Take the boys and get out for a change, he offered. It's a family event full of food booths and entertainment. The thought of an evening watching Dumbo or Pinocchio for the umpteenth time cinched the deal. If he'd heard about my altercation with Malibu Barbie, he was kind enough not to bring it up and spare me further embarrassment.

"Just make sure you only walk on the main streets with lights, don't go down any alleys." Manuel adjusted his tool belt and wiped the sweat off his forehead. I tensed at the upcoming onslaught of horrific daily news, but he seemed to sense my fragile state and instead said many of the neighbors would be heading out around six for dinner. I nodded, appreciative of his restraint.

We showered, dressed, and Ricardo and Agustín skipped next to me as we made up silly songs. They ran up ahead a few yards, and turned the corner.

Agustín gasped. "Mami, hurry! Come and see."

The boys clapped in awe.

I caught up to the shimmering park strung with hundreds of lights, dozens of food booths scattered along the walkways, families sitting on blankets, and children running around while clowns juggled and music serenaded the night. I knelt down to take it in from their perspective and then took their hands firmly in mine as we joined the people of Juárez in their summer festivities. We greeted people, checked out every food booth, and found thinly sliced grilled beef and chicken piled high onto soft rolls for tortas that were topped with avocados, onions, and marinated roasted chiles; rows of roasted corn on the cob sprinkled with coarse Mexican cheese; cups brimming with chunks of pineapple, watermelon, cucumber, jicama, and mango drenched in lemon; multi-colored swirls of cotton candy; greasy bags of warm popcorn; and tall paper cups of ice cold limonada, horchata, and tamarindo, all for a few pesos. After a thorough inspection I decided to buy from the vendors who had jugs of bottled water and the longest lines.

We didn't have a blanket, but found a soft patch of grass underneath a tree and set out our assortment of steaming food and sweet rice and cinnamon drinks.

"I did this very same thing with my family. We'll do it with Papi soon," I said.

The warm summer night filled me with nostalgia for the early sixties when life in Nogales, Arizona, included our devoted grandparents, who ruled the roost with unconditional love. The boys devoured every morsel of food, burped, and sat back rubbing their full bellies. A motley group of kids were making up teams and beckoned my oldest to join in. To my surprise he didn't hesitate, and for a while I forgot my fear and regrets, watching their joy. Agustín playing tag among a group of giggling kids and Ricardo's slobbery smile when a piece of cotton candy melted in his mouth.

It seemed every family had a father at their side. I missed Marty. That tiny ache was impossible to dismiss; instead it sprouted tendrils of nagging reminders and wishful thinking. This was all so different from what I had imagined doing when I became a mother. No bottle feedings, no first steps, or words, no first birthdays. No indulgently raising one child at a time. Marty often reminded me of the reality of having an infant. We're ahead of the game, he'd say, no diaper bags, strollers, and grimy pacifiers, and most important of all, no round two of the adoption process. We're done. Remember, we're older parents and we've made up for lost time. Had we?

We walked home with a bunch of balloons trailing behind us in a group of other families headed in our direction. Manuel had found us while we were watching the clowns juggle, introduced us to his family, and then quietly asked me not to walk home alone.

Agustín wanted to know why Marty wasn't with us as we climbed the stairs to our apartment. He had noticed some children on their fathers' shoulders, other fathers pulling out money to buy the food or rounding up their brood to leave the park.

He's working back at home, I explained, but assured him he'd be with us soon.

"When?" Agustín wasn't satisfied with my usual reply.

I put up five fingers as I opened the door and ushered them in.

He asked me to show him again. I fanned out my fingers and counted each one.

"¿Cinco?" He repeated. I nodded. He then went to the bunch of balloons and asked me to count out five balloons. We did together.

Hours later I awoke startled. Ricardo was moaning. I scrambled to find my glasses, my hands sticky with sweat.

The stand-up fan in my bedroom circulated hot, stale air. Ricardo sat up in bed, hair matted, and T-shirt soaked in perspiration. Agustín rubbed his eyes and fanned out his T-shirt as he lethargically rocked his head back and forth.

Cursing under my breath, I went into the living room. The only vent in the apartment verified the pitiful swamp cooler had stopped working. Turning the switch off and saying three quick Hail Mary's before turning it back on didn't produce a miracle, not even a sputter of tepid air. I threw open curtains and windows in all of the rooms, wincing at the blast of sirens and traffic. The boys' guzzled tumblers of ice water while I mopped their faces and bodies with towels, but beads of sweat appeared seconds later. A cool shower helped us rebound, but within minutes, as I changed their sheets, perspiration dripped from my underarms and breasts. It had been one hundred and twenty degrees at the peak of the day. The night felt like Death Valley.

The boys were wide-awake and glistening as I fanned them with large sheets of construction paper. I knew from our CPR classes that dehydration in children could be fatal. We went to the refrigerator door for the pitcher of ice water. The boys sighed in relief as the cool air reached our bodies. The hell with it, I thought, dismissing the waste of energy and propping the door open. I grabbed a blanket, laid it right in front of the refrigerator, and let the boys bask in the cool air while I leaned against the cupboards. I scanned the contents of the refrigerator shelves and laid eyes on a bowl of grape Jell-O. The boys opened their mouths like tiny birds and I spooned the sparkly gelatin onto their tongues. They closed their eyes as their mouths exploded with cool sweetness. Agustín patted his stomach after each spoonful while I wiped purple drool from Ricardo's chin until the bowl was empty.

When Agustín got up to gather a pile of books for me to read, he noticed the furniture piled up against one wall. Why had I moved the furniture around, he asked, hands on hips. Didn't I know we couldn't open the door? How would we get out? How would Papi get in? I bonked my forehead with the butt of my open hand and said I'd forgotten to put it all back after I did my exercises. My eldest demanded, his arms crossed at his chest, I show him just what exercise meant. Sheesh. He nodded his approval after a set of push-ups, sit-ups, some aerobic prancing, and a yoga pretzel pose as the grand finale. Convinced, Agustín walked back to the blanket and made his first book request: *Where is Spot?*

Once I went through the stack of books, Agustín stood up and offered to sing as Ricardo laid his head on my thighs. He entertained us with some Barney songs that sounded much better in Spanish, and then went on to a song about a mother duck and her five ducklings, and "Las Mañanitas," México's version of "Happy Birthday." Ricardo and I clapped and cheered after each song while Agustín bowed. Pure ham and cheese, this son of mine.

"I was very shy as a little girl and wouldn't have been brave enough to sing alone in front of anyone," I said.

Agustín beamed and then asked Ricardo to sing a song, but his little brother only burrowed closer to me. He finally felt cool. I was wondering whether to cut up some watermelon or pineapple when I remembered the treat in the freezer. We watched a video as I placed a frozen M&M on their tongues. They scrunched up their shoulders in delight while Mary Poppins flew through the air, singing and magically tidying up the children's bedroom. Towards the end of the movie Ricardo fell asleep as the pre-dawn air cooled off.

A new bond had formed between us. I felt like a bona fide mother. We went to bed and slept in for the first time.

The next morning while Manuel was on the roof repairing the cooler motor, Agustín asked me when Papi would arrive, and Ricardo put up his five fingers. I put up four fingers. Agustín went to the balloons and asked me to count out four balloons. We now had one too many. I took one out of the bunch, covered Ricardo's car, and popped the extra balloon. They cheered. We started our day each morning by popping a balloon and we were thrilled when we popped the last balloon and knew that Marty's arrival day had come.

August 14th

> *Even though Marty stayed longer then usual, his visit seemed to pass too quickly. He arrived like Santa Claus with bags of groceries from El Paso, books, magazines, and a pile of videos. We caught the tail end of a news report with an update on the serial killer: almost 100 deaths. He is stalking, raping, and brutally murdering young women going to work in American factories. That's followed by a report on the marauding gypsies who are targeting Juárez and a warning not to open the door to any stranger day or night. Lovely.*

The next time I spoke with Marty on the phone, he delivered good news. Claudia was coming to visit in a few days. My niece had broken up with her boyfriend and needed to lick her wounds. I swooned at the thought of help and company. I loved feeling the fullness of carrying the boys, but my small frame complained when I collapsed into bed each night.

Three days later, the boys and I sat on the shaded balcony rolling a ball between us while watching new tenants move in downstairs. Three clean-shaven young men waved up at the boys as they carried in labeled boxes and suitcases. I tossed the ball farther and the boys chased after it, laughter, and squeals rolling off their shoulders as they reached the top of the stairs.

"Hello." A hand reached out from the top of the stairs and swatted the ball in the other direction. The boys were startled for only a moment then turned after the ball coming back my way.

A second voice followed. Two of my neighbors, a couple of young, harried housewives who rented apartments at the opposite end of the building, were balancing shopping bags in one hand and Popsicles in the other.

I introduced us as I grabbed a couple of bulging plastic bags. Yvonne, the mother of two toddlers, remarked how no one would guess they were married since they did so much on their own.

Olga, the older one with a pair of teenagers, rubbed the red crease on her arm and bemoaned that they looked like pack mules as she led me into her apartment. In a nutshell, she explained their husbands were business consultants from out of town. They came along expecting a house with a swimming pool and maids. The husbands were working twenty-hour days, staying at a downtown hotel while they were relegated to sub-standard Suites Victoria.

I envied their companionship, their ability to bolster one another. We exchanged information and they promised to visit us soon.

We went back to the balcony to wait for my niece, blowing bubbles, watching them float away until they popped. Every time we saw a taxi at the corner we stood up and waved, hoping it was Claudia. Finally the fourth taxi slowed down and turned into the parking lot. I took the boys by their hands and we ran downstairs to greet their cousin.

"I thought Phoenix was hot." Claudia shot out of the taxi and wrapped her arms around me as the boys tugged at my shirt and shorts.

"Don't look now, but we're in hell." I joked. "In case you haven't noticed, these are my sons, Agustín and Ricardo."

"Ahh, they're so cute." She knelt down, introduced herself, and hugged them. They each shook her hand and repeated their name. Then they insisted on taking her suitcase and dragged it along the walkway as we tripped over each other's words.

"I'm glad you're raising a pair of gentlemen." Claudia put her arm around me. "Are you all right? Have you been sick?"

"I've had a sinus infection, but overall I've been fine. Why?"

"Because you are way too thin," she remarked, as she looked me over. "Now, don't get me wrong. I'd like to know your secret. I've been eating way too many pints of Ben & Jerry's lately."

"It's easy. Adopt two kids and live in this armpit during the summer."

After putting the boys to bed, my twenty-four year old niece took out her deck of cards and we played several rounds of Gin Rummy before I broached the touchy subject of her break-up. She waved my question away, said she wasn't ready to talk about it, and instead wanted me to tell her all about Juárez. I apologized that it was not a tourist town and our stay didn't feel like a vacation. I was relieved when my niece said she didn't care, because all she wanted to do was hang around with us. This was music to my ears. As she expertly shuffled the cards for another round of cards we heard a thump.

"What was that?" Claudia looked around startled.

"Ricardo," I answered as I looked over my cards. "He falls off the bed almost every night," I said and got up to check on him.

"That's wild. He doesn't even cry?"

"Because I put pillows down on his side the bed, so he doesn't fall on the floor, plus he's a sound sleeper." Sure enough my baby was snoring contentedly on a pile of pillows and didn't rouse when I put him back into bed.

"You're pretty blasé about it," Claudia chuckled in disbelief.

"Oh, I freaked out the first time he hit the floor screaming, the poor little guy. Since I couldn't figure out a way to keep him in bed, I made his fall safer." The fatigue crashed down on my lighthearted act. I was so ready to unload all of my fears and worries and have a good cry, but she was my niece, so I reined it back in and played cards.

At midnight I refused to play another round, reminding her of my sons, who were early risers. I stretched, stood up, and asked her to help me move the furniture.

"You're kidding?" She continued shuffling and fanning the cards.

"Nope," I recounted the headline news in Juárez as we pushed the sofa against the door.

"Why don't you ask the manager to replace the lock with a dead bolt?" She was perplexed.

"Because the doors are hollow. Doors with dead bolts and wrought-iron bars haven't stopped them. This way, they can't push the door open, an inch, even if they do break the lock." I heaved and shoved the end table into place with my feet.

"Do you have mace?" Claudia said.

"Yes."

"Shit. How do you sleep at night?"

"I really don't. I'm getting used to it." Claudia hugged me. I ate it up.

We spent the next couple of days watching videos and playing cards. Claudia was determined to win, but I was having incredible luck. Going to bed much later equaled waking up more tired and cranky. I noticed Claudia, like Jannette, wasn't asking how she could help with the boys, and instead read from her pile of *People* magazines, watched TV, and napped. I was envious. I had to ask her to read to them, to help them get dressed or finish a jigsaw puzzle. Why had I expected my family to come equipped with the mindfulness to know I now needed help? I was no longer just a sister or an aunt. Why'd I think my years of pampering them would've automatically garnered me payback in the form of ideal baby sitter? My silent complaints turned into resentment. It took years for me to recognize that I could've taken responsibility and asked for help, delegated, and shown them how to pitch in. Jannette and Claudia weren't mothers or mind readers.

When we arrived from our morning swim on the third day we rousted Claudia off of the sofa with an offer for lunch. I wanted her to sample a true burrito: a freshly made, fluffy, hubcap-sized tortilla filled with chile Colorado or delicate green chile rellenos without the mushy rice, lettuce, sour cream, cabbage, or other fillers that Americans used to make their "Super Burrito."

I put the boys in the shower and as I bent down to lather them up, I felt dizzy and lightheaded. I hadn't eaten my usual rolls with my coffee.

"Claudia," I called out as I rinsed Ricardo. "Do me a favor?"

She stood by the doorway, brushing her hair.

"I'm feeling a bit dizzy. Would you dry and diaper Ricardo while I get a drink of water?" I grabbed a towel and wrapped it around his little body and helped him out of the shower stall. Agustín was entertaining himself by blowing bubbles with a mixture of snot and soap.

"Sure." Claudia took my place.

I left for the kitchen while Claudia danced with Ricardo into their bedroom. I pressed the cool glass against my forehead, when I heard a loud gasp.

"Oh, my God. I can not deal with this."

Ricardo must of peed or pooped on her while she was putting on his diaper.

"His penis. Something is wrong with his penis." She stood in the bedroom doorway with one hand covering her eyes.

I squeezed by her and ran to the bed imagining the worst. Why hadn't I noticed while I was giving him a shower? Had he hurt it in the pool? Was it bleeding? Ricardo was sitting up, smearing the drool on his chest with the diaper laying flat next to him. His penis looked fine.

"What's wrong with it, Claudia?"

"Look." She refused to remove her hand from her eyes. "Look at it." My niece pointed an accusatory index finger at Ricardo's chubby thighs.

Then it hit me. His penis wasn't circumcised. He had extra flesh covering the tip. I explained to her that most Mexican boys didn't have their penis circumcised.

"Well, that's simply awful."

"No, it's not. And, please, don't make that face in front of them. There is nothing wrong with their penises. I'll put his diaper on, but you go get Agustín out of the shower for me."

"Is his penis the same?"

"Oh for God's sake, Claudia. I need help." I whimpered as a headache hammered the back of my neck. "Now get a grip and get the kid out of the shower."

She somehow managed to do so without taking her eyes off of Agustín's face and chest. I made fun of her naiveté the rest of her visit and told her she better make sure she checked out her next boyfriend's penis because circumcision was not universal.

At the end of the week, I was sad and relieved when Claudia left. On the second night, I yearned to see her dealing cards at the tiny living room table, a pitcher of limonada and a bowl of potato chips sprinkled with hot sauce by her side. I'd berate myself for being so critical, forgetting she was young, and had only one brother. Not everyone helped raise a wagon full of siblings.

Ms. D called, and Manuel was kind enough to bring his portable phone to me while we were at the pool. The magistrate had just told her the petition had been in Chihuahua City for a few days. Next, it would be approved and sent on to México City and then back in Juárez by the middle of September. We could make it out of here before the end of the month.

August 26th

We continue to pop balloons and wait for Marty. Waiting has taken on a new meaning for me; it now has a personality: it's the boring neighbor who comes to visit you at the wrong time of day and doesn't take a hint that you want them to leave. As the visit draws on and your discomfort heightens and would be visible to any other person, the visitor takes off their shoes, tucks their feet in on the sofa, and settles in to drone on and on about their life and not once ask a question about yours.

Thanks to the Oprah Show I'm now meditating before I go to sleep and it is helping calm me down. I hope it helps with the nightmares.

I'm so superstitious that I won't write down these dreams, am afraid that they might come true.

It's after two in the morning; my heart is pounding out of my chest. Some random noise woke me up. I went to the kitchen to drink water and I heard voices outside. I carefully peeked around the curtain and saw a big truck parked out on the street. Seconds later the street lamp was smashed. I went to the living room window and could make out silhouettes moving around. *What the heck is going on?* I don't dare turn any lights on so I'm in the bathroom with a flashlight and the door closed as I write.

I take three aspirin and rub more Arnica on my back, but the pain is intensifying and my nerves are raw.

I go to bed, but I can't sleep. I wait for another sound. I wait for relief from my back pain. I wait for daylight. I wait for Marty. I wait for the judges. I wait for the petition. Wait, negate, late, mate, fate, bait, date, rate, gate, placate, exacerbate, investigate, emulate, masticate, escalate, fornicate.

I just want to go home with my sons before something does happen to us.

W = wallow

A = anxious

I = impatient

T = tempest

I = inferno

N = neglect

G = gnaw

CHAPTER XVI

SEPTEMBER 1998

The highlight of the week: discovering another pay phone across the street from Suites Victoria. Odd, I hadn't seen it before, right in plain sight. A clean, working phone with no line of foot-tapping, throat clearing people around it. Pretty pathetic, but this brightened my mood. Luckily, a hefty cloud cloaking the early morning sun cast a protective shadow making my task bearable. Catching Ms. D before other families and paperwork consumed her time kept me awake half the night searching for a hint of daylight coming through my window. Now, I sat the boys on the sidewalk, flush against a wall, each with a book in hand to keep them from wandering into traffic. A threat of a time out replaced

the usual bribe of bubble gum or candy now that the consequences of straying were far worse than Baja Barbie beating
me up.

I'd broken my vow to be different than my parents when
I'd spanked Agustín, a few days earlier, for running ahead
and crossing the street oblivious of the cars speeding right
at him. A guardian angel must have helped him reach the
sidewalk unscathed. Cars slammed on their brakes, drivers letting me cross the street while they chastised me for
my recklessness. Panic-stricken, I bounded after him and
clamped his body to mine with my free hand while I repositioned Ricardo on my hip. Kneeling down, I pointed out
the danger and reminded him of the rules. He nodded and
took off across the street again. I snatched his T-shirt as
his feet flew off the curb, lost control, and spanked him.
He gasped then wailed. I thought my hand would shrivel.
I apologized and promised never to touch him in anger
again, but the sticky film of guilt remained. Even though,
later that day, my mother-in-law absolved me for the whack
on his behind, I knew I had unleashed a little of my own
mother. I now treaded on shaky ground.

Timing was crucial and the line for the phone by the
pool struck at my last nerve. I'd missed Ms. D by minutes
one too many times. Not today. Bleary-eyed and cranky, I
dialed the DIF phone number by heart, pretending Snow
White cheerfulness when the receptionist greeted me by my
first name and transferred me to Ms. D straight away. Her
abrupt manner was a welcome change, leaving me a wide
berth to rapid fire questions and scribble in short hand as
she bullet listed her most recent information. The last item
was the gold nugget I'd been mining for—the petition had

made it to the capitol. I held my breath. Kept one eye and ear on the boys. One judge down, three to go. According to her sources it would take at least a month if not six weeks to get approved. A huge backlog, plus the upcoming sixteenth of September festivities marking independence from Spain, a national holiday, would stall our petition. I coiled the phone cord around my wrist and up my arm.

"My source at family court says maybe a bit of oil will help the machinery," Ms. D said stretching and snapping oil into two syllables.

"Marty and I made a pact we wouldn't bribe anyone, no matter how tempting." For a split second paranoia crept in. Was she setting us up? Could she be the wolf in a pastel pantsuit?

"I'm sorry."

"Don't be, it's just too risky." I deliberately made a point to repeat our stance on the off chance the phone call was being recorded.

When I called Marty, he doubted Ms. D's suggestion hinted at deception, but was relieved I hadn't taken the bait, just in case. We were scraping the bottom of the idea barrel when Marty reminded me of the woman I'd met in a class months before leaving for Juárez. Stirred by our determination, she'd handed me her Mexican ex-husband's name and phone number. Once I arrived, she implored, call Enrique. He'd do anything for her, their parting was amicable, but foremost, he had connections in México City.

"Everybody says they have connections in México City." I changed the subject. I disliked cold calling strangers for favors, but I hated living here more. Plus my husband sounded like a death row inmate requesting his last meal.

I called Enrique, introduced myself to his secretary, explained my primitive phone situation, and pitched her my situation. At least I'd tried, but as Oprah reminded her viewers, I kept my expectation level to non-existent.

By mid-morning the water seemed a touch cooler when I joined Ricardo on the second step of the pool to watch Agustín swim underwater, from one end of the narrow pool to the other. Manuel surprised me with his portable phone. It was Enrique.

My acquaintance with his ex-wife gave me carte blanche to his time and help. We chatted like old friends; he congratulated me on our progress, told me to hang on, he'd do whatever possible to get us out of Juárez. He was leaving for Europe, but would call an old friend who happened to be a high-powered lawyer in D.F., the capital. This person would contact me later today. I thanked him, but didn't hold my breath. I didn't bother to call Marty.

Once back in the apartment, I checked in on the boys who were splashing in a few inches of water in the shower. I prepared a pot of rice and lowered the burner to a simmer when Manuel knocked on the door and then tapped the kitchen window with the portable phone. He sported a fresh haircut glistening with pomade, his mustache reminiscent of Yosemite Sam's in black. His voice was nearly drowned out by the vendor hawking red and green chile tamales with the aid of a megaphone.

The voice on the phone wasn't familiar, and when she addressed me by my formal name I immediately tensed up. What was wrong now?

"I'm María, Enrique's friend."

I turned off the stove, peeked in on the boys, and retreated to the bedroom, where I gave her a detailed synopsis of the process, what we had accomplished, what was still left to do, and where we needed help.

"Do you know how rare it is for an American couple to adopt a Mexican child?" María asked.

"Only four successful adoptions in the last five years."

"You've done your homework." María perked up.

"And then some."

"The numbers are grim, but it's not impossible to do." Her voice was upbeat as she asked for more details, but gasped when I told her Marty was commuting from Northern California and I lived alone in Juárez.

Before we got off the phone she gave me her office, cell, and home phone numbers and told me repeatedly that she was going to dedicate herself to getting our petition approved as soon as possible. I could call her anytime, even if it was just to vent. She'd call me as soon as she located our petition. I not only thanked her and bestowed her with best wishes, but also blessed her and her entire family. When she hung up, I dropped my face onto my knees, hugged myself into a tight little ball, and wept.

After lunch I put the boys down for their nap and succumbed to drawing a September calendar grid that resembled a blank tic-tac-toe game. I looked over at the expired June, July, and August calendars brimming with arrows pointing to dates of anticipated deadlines, circles around numbers signified holidays when nothing would happen and numbers decorated with stars signaled Marty's arrival. Now all of those numbers had been crossed out heavily before the entire calendar was scribbled over. This would be the last calendar I'd draw. Maybe I'd only fill in half of the month with numbers. Optimism? Denial?

Once the boys got up from their nap, we went to the corner market and used our favorite pay phone outside the store where an ample patio kept the boys away from traffic and lines were non-existent. After installing the boys underneath the red-and-white striped metal awning with a lollipop bribe and strict instructions not to budge an inch, I inserted my phone card and kept an eagle eye on them.

"Don't get your hopes up too high," Marty warned as I talked a mile a minute, recounting my conversation with M. "It could take her days to find the petition and that's if she manages to find someone who sympathizes with our case. Don't expect too much to happen right away."

"I know all that, but if you had heard her you'd know what I mean. Please don't burst my bubble." Desperation fueled my hope.

"You're right. It is the best news we've had in a long time. Call me when you hear from her again."

"Just think next time you come down could be the last time."

"Could be," was all Marty would say.

We took the long way to Suites Victoria and I made up stories about the people who lived in the pale blue house with the lime green papier-mâché parrot hanging in the window. Agustín stopped in his tracks and wanted to see the miniature family who flew from room to room on the parrot for himself. How did I know, he scowled. We'd never visited this house before. If the parrot could fly, why wasn't it flying now? I threw my hands up in the air; eyes bugged out, and whined like a six-year-old that it was a story I'd made up for fun. He squinted his eyes and wagged his little index finger at me. Didn't I know it was a sin to lie? I gave up explaining the difference when he covered his ears. Why did he bug me so much at times? Poor little guy was just being a kid.

I turned off the light well after midnight and stared out the small thin-paned bedroom window. The fan was on low now. Sirens circled the block. Toilets flushed, furniture moved, conversations started and ended as I inventoried my day. The shattering of glass dispatched a hand underneath the pillow for the mace and with the other grabbed my glasses. Like a military exercise, I jumped to my feet then peeked around my doorway, expecting gunfire or evil incarnate. Please, I prayed, don't let me pass out. Was it the living room or kitchen window? My eyes acclimated to the dark. Nothing moved inside the apartment. I darted to the boys' doorway. Sound asleep. Thank God. I picked up one of their wooden toy trucks with my free hand and almost dropped it when another crash of glass weakened my courage. The faint light against the kitchen curtains faded. The streetlight had been smashed. Again. My heart thundered against my collarbone. My mouth so parched it hurt to swallow. I peeked out from the kitchen curtain. A van was parked out in the street with multiple cars in front and behind it. I let the curtain go and stood against the wall shivering with fright. A door slammed. Motors started. One by one each vehicle drove away until an eerie quiet entombed the neighborhood. Was anyone else crouched behind thin curtains witnessing this along with me? Even though my tongue felt like sandpaper, I didn't dare open the refrigerator. I felt around for the water jug at the end of the counter and remembered the cup by the sink. I drank and held the cup to my chest. The screeching of sirens and howling dogs now calmed me. I'd call Marty as soon as the boys woke up. I fell asleep sitting up in bed, mace in hand.

I finally caught Marty coming back from lunch.

"I don't tell you everything I hear on the news, because I don't want to scare you," he said, "but the drug cartels are feuding over Juárez. All hell is about to break loose! It's making the serial killer look tame in comparison."

"Oh great. I should sleep a whole lot better now that I know that my downstairs neighbors might carve me up like a turkey."

"Just keep out of their way. I don't want them noticing you. All right?"

"You said we'd be celebrating your birthday in Santa Cruz," I said instead of answering his question.

"And I hate that I'm fucking wrong." Seconds later we hung up. I stuck my tongue out at the pay phone, wishing Marty would materialize like Captain Kirk with his transporter, so I could pick a fight. Instead we walked around the complex while I stewed.

Three months into this process and we'd only scaled half of the mountainous hurdles. We couldn't even begin the passports, INS, and American Consulate requirements until our petition was approved. What had I been thinking of when I agreed to this? I just had to be a mother. I couldn't accept life without children. Someone else in their right mind might have seen the writing on the wall, been clued in after miscarriages, ectopic pregnancies, and a failed adoption that it just wasn't meant to be and made peace with their fate. Not me, a pitiful and exhausted forty-five-year-old woman raising two little boys who deserved their own young mother. My thoughts blackened into a tornado spiraling out of control and flattening, in its wake, my best intentions, and hopes, leaving me crushed with despair. I deserved this for being so stubborn and hard headed. What in the fuck was I doing here? Just tell Marty, I thought. Tell someone. Admit my mistake. Accept failure. Just when I'd resolved to tell my mother-in-law for starters, my demons, the traffic noise, and blaring radios seemed to quiet, leaving the boys' gasps of laughter poised in the air. The tornado lifted its destructive tail and shifted away, allowing me a glimpse of providence orchestrating something bigger than me.

I sank down against the bright pink wall, chuckling at their goofy attempts at a piggyback ride from the white ceramic lions at the entrance of the complex. Manuel came around the corner, wiping his brow with his handkerchief, motioning to a crew of painters who disappeared into a vacant apartment. He tore out a single sheet from his note-pad and blushed after I gave him a big hug in thanks. María had called back and was waiting for my phone call. We headed for the phone by the pool. I figured Ms. Gold Lamé was awake by now, and instructed the boys to stay right by my side. When no one was latched onto the phone, I took it as a good omen.

I pictured María dressed in an exquisitely tailored suit, pacing on Italian high heels as she spoke.

"I spoke a few minutes on the phone with the Secretary of State, who assured me your petition was in good hands. He gave me the name of who to contact, so I spent the morning at the adoption court with his young, beautifully groomed assistants."

My stomach lurched as she painted an all too familiar picture of disorganization and chaos where petitions could be easily lost.

"I left them looking for your petition and returned with coffees and a box of pastries."

She made me laugh at how the inexperienced women clapped and hugged her like little girls receiving a gift for good behavior. This offering allowed María access to the stacks of petitions. In less than an hour she'd helped them sort them by dates received and then alphabetized each stack.

"Then we sorted through several plastic bins of unopened mail where I found the DHL envelope with your petition."

"They wouldn't give me or let me make a copy. I'm sorry, you need to fax me one right away."

I hung up feeling able to shake off some of the scorched funk trailing after me. As we were walking back to the apartment I noticed a scooter with a metal box attached to the back part of the seat pull up to the parking lot. The driver took off his helmet, opened the metal lid, and pulled out a familiar thin square box. Pizza delivery: the answer to dinner. Things were definitely looking up.

When the wiry fellow returned, we approached him. He handed us a flyer, said he prided himself on delivering hot pizzas as he put on his helmet, and sped off. Then I noticed a dilapidated car with New Mexico license plates pull up next to our neighbor's car. The passengers hadn't yet opened the doors when a second car, a van with Texas license plates, drove up. I glanced over at the streetlight. It had been replaced. These folks were here to make a pick up. I wondered if the streetlight would be smashed again tonight and these cars would leave shortly after. I hurried the boys along and got them into the apartment just in time for the *Oprah* show.

A couple of hours later, when I opened the door for the pizza delivery guy, I caught a glimpse of a police car double parked downstairs. Two policemen, my neighbors, and some of their friends leaned against the car drinking beer and cracking jokes. Nothing new.

The next day we took a taxi to DIF, picked up the petition from la Recepciónista, who radiated purple from eye shadow to stilettos. I hightailed it in the same taxi to the mall where, after several attempts, I found a stationary store that had a working fax machine.

The boss was out and the two young clerks fumbled over themselves to figure out how to work the machine. Meanwhile Ricardo toppled a tall display that sent notebooks and pens flying everywhere and Agustín kept smearing a glass case with his tongue, from one end to the other.

What seemed like hours later, the storeowner took me aside and apologized for the clerk's mishaps. He'd gotten the gist of our document and offered me a huge discount. He gifted the boys a glittery pencil then took my hand in both of his and said God would bless us for life. I choked up at his kind words and generosity and gave him a hoarse thank you. I went back to the pay phone and confirmed with María. She indeed had the complete petition in her hands.

September 6th

Right on cue minutes after we pushed the furniture against the front door and went to bed the streetlight was smashed. I grabbed Marty

and he covered my mouth. I was whimpering as
he got out of bed, went to the window and a few
minutes later came back. He promised me that we
would be out of here soon. It took us a long time
to get to sleep.

The changes were evident as mid-September drew near: the boys now wore pajamas to bed every night, we spent mornings at the park and swam only in the afternoon, we stopped turning on the swamp cooler and fans, and *Oprah's* fall season began.

This week she had a special guest, Dr. John Grey, of *Men are From Mars and Women are From Venus* fame, to discuss and work through the obstacles keeping us from attaining our goals. He highlighted four emotions that accompany us through life: anger, sadness, fear, and sorrow. Speaking passionately how we had the power to change our lives with our thoughts and actions. Easy for you to say, I thought, you don't live in Juárez. He brought up an audience member and had her work through the steps with him. First she had to identify her obstacles. I wrote "impatience" for mine. He then stacked several big plastic blocks and had the woman physically smash her obstacle away.

I found two empty plastic water jugs and laid one on its side to stack them, then borrowed Agustín's plastic bat to smash my impatience away. I swung hard and sent the jug across the room into the sofa with a heavy thud. It felt good. I repositioned the jugs as Dr. Grey told the woman to swing harder and give it all she had. She held up the bat with her pinky in the air and tapped a bit harder.

I placed the bat high up behind my head, swiveled my hips, and swung with full force as I said, "I destroy my impatience." I took the applause from the audience as mine and followed up with a dramatic bow. Next I created a new affirmation. I wrote in large block letters: I live in courage. I retraced the letters over and over until the ink bled onto the next page. I slept without clenching my fists.

A few days later, Ms. D called. The petition was back in Juárez for the final review and approval.

"Remember, tomorrow is a national holiday and many people take off an extra day." She paused. "Then the petition needs to be recorded to issue the boys their new birth certificates with your last names."

The sound of their names—Agustín and Ricardo Raptis Picco—injected renewed hope.

I counted out days and projected it was quite possible to get all the requirements and leave before the end of September. I could begin packing some things next week. I told the boys that we'd be going home soon. They clapped and cheered, we all danced around the apartment.

The next morning, we woke up early, got dressed up, and headed out for the Sixteenth of September parade and festivities. Families were out in droves setting up their lawn chairs and blankets under shady trees and awnings to celebrate Mexico's hard-won independence from Spain. The sun was tame, the air balmy, and the mood boisterous as Mexican flags decorated every lamppost, window, and free hand. Agustín skipped alongside as I carried Ricardo. The boys waved their flags over their heads as we walked down the boulevard, taking in new sights and passing new restaurants, where wafts of home cooking slowed us down.

We found a shady block under a cluster of lush Jacaranda trees heavy with lavender blooms, where a large family immediately welcomed and made space for us. The elders coaxed Agustín and Ricardo toward the curb where they could stand or sit comfortably to watch the upcoming parade. After I introduced myself, Agustín took us by surprise as he formally introduced himself and shook everyone's hand.

Ricardo refused to budge from behind my legs. I loved feeling the boys around me, holding my hand, hugging my knees, or leaning their heads against my hips. I didn't recall doing this with my mother, but I remembered being Agustín's age, trying to get settled in before the marching band's drums echoed down the street.

I recalled the excitement, the giddiness, and the mammoth parade floats coming from across the border on Calle Obregón into Grand Avenue where it seemed every person in town was present.

Ricardo jolted and grabbed me when the first round of drums and trumpets exploded close by.

I was overcome with childhood memories when two countries opened up their borders for the multicultural pageantry of marching bands, cavalries, mariachis, majorettes tossing batons overhead, and red, green, white, and blue festooned parade floats where the queen and her court threw confetti and streamers into the crowds. I fought back tears remembering my pack of siblings, toes lined up and perched at the edge of the sidewalk, straining for a peek at our father decked out in cowboy attire chauffeuring some politician in his champagne-colored Lincoln Continental convertible grinning ear to ear and waving back at folks, but pointing and winking at us. I'd left my brothers and sisters to follow him down a few blocks, convinced he had stolen the politician's thunder with his drop-dead gorgeous good looks and movie star smile. After the parade when folks were heading home, I'd join my siblings at our grandparents' restaurant, the Triangle Café, right on Grand Avenue, on the same block as the police and fire station where all of the action was, literally. The restaurant was our home away from home, where we'd take over the family booth, fight over the comic section, and drink coffee with our pancakes.

Now, my sons watched everyone else's reaction as closely as they did the parade, clapping, yelling out "Bravo," and waving their flags overhead as the pageantry swept by. Would they remember this as vividly?

September 19th

> *We went to Sanborn's for breakfast to celebrate that we crossed off another step and are closer to getting home. Turned the corner to Suites Victoria when we saw our street blocked off completely by what I thought were police, but in fact were the P.J.F., Federal Swat team. It seems that our quiet low-profile patriarch across the street was a drug and weapons dealer who the P.J.F. had been pursuing for some time. Manuel told me to make ourselves scarce. The P.J.F. was questioning everybody and he didn't want the boys to be scared. We spent hours at the park before heading back to the apartment.*

I went out of my way to avoid headlines with the words *murder*, *assault*, *kidnap*, *rape*, *serial killer*, or *burglary*, Fear paralyzed me. I felt jinxed, trapped. Edgy. I'd become a shrew. Scolding the boys for little things that never mattered before, squeezing their arm tighter than necessary to get their attention, and threatening to spank them when they misbehaved. My apologies felt forced and I could see my mother rolling her eyes at me.

I'd jerk awake at night, recalling the threatening men in camouflage and flak jackets, armed with bulky weapons. Drug cartels. *Desaparecidas*. Young women. Young girls. Mothers. Daughters. Sisters and aunts devoured in broad daylight, on their way to or from work, and left to rot in the desert.

I patrolled the apartment. Checked on the boys. Peeked out each window. Stared at the streets. Sidewalks. Trees. I trained my eyes on each centimeter as I scanned my view from the far left side, counting to sixty as I made my way over to the right and back again. Over and over. The wind rattled the windows. My feet hurt. My back complained. Before going back to bed, I placed a plastic lamp on top of the furniture against the front door, figuring it hitting the tile floor would alert me if the door were pried open. I'd have a few seconds more to grab the mace under my pillow and the baseball bat next to the bed and protect my children. I now slept with my glasses on.

CHAPTER XVII

SEPTEMBER 1998

A few days later, we received the boys' birth certificates. I called Marty as I danced a tango with the phone cord. He made his plane reservation. I gave notice on the apartment. What a great feeling. I broke out in a permanent goofy grin. We were going home.

Marty arrived to another celebration with streamers and giddy fun, but first thing the next morning, we planned out each step and double-checked every slip of paper in our bulging expandable portfolio. By seven thirty the following morning, we shook off the chill as we waited our turn in line to present our passport applications.

"I can't believe we're finally here." I put my arm around Marty's waist while he carried Ricardo and I had Agustín on the other side.

"I can't believe how smoothly the line is moving," Marty added. We reached the front of the line and handed over our two neat stacks. An older woman explained that it would take an hour or so for the passport officer to speak with us. If everything were in order, we'd have the passports after 3:00 p.m. that same day.

We found chairs at the back of the room so that the boys could move around. My harshness with the boys diminished when Marty was present. Was it his help that made the difference or trepidation he'd see my unsavory family habits reveal themselves?

"I hope we go home today," I whispered.

"The worst case is we spend the night in El Paso and leave first thing tomorrow." Marty took my hands in his and kissed them. "We're almost home, baby." We went over our busy day, and the next few, into the following week, when Marty would take time off to be with us at home.

"Did you hear our name? Or am I hearing things?" I sat up and leaned toward the front of the room where the officers stood to call out the applicants' names.

"You heard right. Let's go."

At five minutes to eight o'clock we were face-to-face with a passport administrator.

"Good morning, Mr. and Ms. Picco. Where did you receive these applications?"

"Here." I answered. I scanned the application and nothing had been checked in red. A good sign.

"When?"

I glanced at Marty before answering, "The middle of July. Why?" My skin began to prick.

The expression on her face matched the gravity of her news. The clerk had given us an outdated application by mistake. The passport requirements for an adopted child to reside in a foreign country had changed the week before we'd walked into the Passport Office, in mid-July and the new forms weren't available.

"What? Impossible." Marty put Ricardo down by his legs and threw his hands up in to the air. "No way!"

"Hold on. Let me talk with her." I held on to the counter, fighting back an urge to scream myself.

"No fucking way. That's not our problem." Marty yelled and everyone in the room went quiet. Every single person pivoted towards us. Please, let the floor part and swallow me up. My heart sank around my ankles. My underarms trickled with sweat.

"Please don't," I said. Agustín and Ricardo were staring at Marty, eyebrows pinched, chins quivering.

Marty's voice remained a steady growl as he leaned over the counter into the woman's face and demanded to speak to the person who could clear this up so that we could go home. He pointed at everyone behind the long counter, taunting the responsible party to come forward.

A young woman appeared to explain and apologized once again.

"Liz, tell her to get her supervisor. It shouldn't be our fault that they fucked up."

"They changed applications and procedures in July, Marty. It's no one's fault. Back off. Please. You're scaring the boys and making it worse," I hissed.

My husband stared back with a rabid look. "Just let me get in front of her supervisor and then I'll go."

"She is the supervisor. Take the boys outside. Please." I bent down and told the boys everything was all right and that Papi would get them a surprise. I gently steered Marty away from the counter and turned back to Ms. G, the supervisor. I profusely apologized for Mary's outburst, explaining we had not only packed all of our belongings, but had given notice on the apartment and were expecting to leave for California tonight, tomorrow morning at the latest.

She nodded, but made sure I understood we still had this untenable situation. International adoptions required that the passport application be reviewed and approved in México City. No exceptions. Translation: another six to eight-week wait. Ms. G handed me a tissue then the new list of requirements on two legal-sized sheets of paper. Our international application would be the first one processed in her office, so we'd have to bear with them as they figured it out. Bile somersaulted in my stomach and stung my esophagus. She asked me to return after three o'clock when they were officially closed. She would help us then. I should use their side entrance, but to please not return before three o'clock.

In the meantime we returned to Suites Victoria where Manuel helped us negotiate a weekly rate. I went into the bathroom and cried while I ran the water. Then we found a bakery and returned with a huge, decadent cake for Manuel.

True to her word, Ms. G ushered us into her office, at a quarter past three, apologizing for the bureaucracy, then in a casual tone explained how we'd create the new application.

She lifted her hands like a conductor and motioned for us to begin. Together. Right now.

"Here's the fax from México City. We need to follow this format and use this wording in each paragraph and clause." She gave Marty a passport law book to refer to as we drafted this document following their strict guidelines. This first draft would serve as the prototype for all future international adoption applications. I read each paragraph out loud, and then we examined the old application to see what parts of it we could use to save time. After a few rounds of discussions, Ms. G took a deep breath and began typing as I dictated the bits and pieces paragraph by paragraph. Two hours later we had a complete document. She said we made a good team as she rubbed her tired eyes. I thanked her again.

"It's the very least I can do," Ms. G said then told us she was making a rare exception and sending off our incomplete application packet, because, she reasoned, this was a test run. Ordinarily an international passport application could only be sent out to México City if every original supporting piece of required documentation was attached. She wished us luck in gathering the other documents and told me to return as soon as I had them all. We'd be in Juárez at least another four to six weeks. Marty would leave tomorrow and would wait until I had an update from México City. I was afraid of saying that it couldn't get worse.

CHAPTER XVIII

OCTOBER 1998

October 5th

I awoke from an awful dream that I was slapping Agustín across the face and he merely stood there staring at me without a reaction. I only wanted to hit him harder. I rolled over, haunted by the dream.

After Marty brought coffee to bed, the dreary morning chill persuaded me to make a batch of rice pudding. I'd surprise the boys with my mother's creamy recipe of a favorite childhood dessert. I poured a half-gallon of whole milk into a pot on the stove and measured out a cup of sugar. I flashed on my mother ladling a warm delicate mound of pudding into a bowl, dusting it with cinnamon, and smiling as we wrapped our lips around the spoonful, swooning with pleasure. We'd hand the empty bowl back to her, our fingers overlapping for a few seconds, and receive, like communion, her love, and affection.

I scraped the final cinnamon-sweet spoonful from my second helping when Manuel arrived, out of breath, with the portable phone. I pressed a heaping bowl of rice pudding into his hands before taking the phone.

"I have news, some good, some not," María said. As corny as it sounds, María seemed like an angel of perpetual good news. A warrior angel, who tracked down and shepherded our application from one desk to another with an indubitable calm and determination. So, I wasn't prepared when she explained a new wrinkle in the international process she couldn't navigate around. The boys' new birth certificates needed a special annotation from their birthplace. In Ricardo's case it wasn't a problem. He was born in Ciudad Juárez. Agustín, however, was born in a remote town in central Baja California Sur, hours from the nearest airport.

"If you wait for the Registro Civil folks to send the birth certificate," María warned, "you could be in Juárez until Christmas."

My neck muscles spasmed, my chest constricted as she described how clerks waited for weeks, even a month or more, until a hefty amount of documents were collected, to send them onto La Paz, Baja California Sur's capital. Then they'd trickle out to small towns and villages and take twice as long to return. Torture. Without hesitation she recommended one of us go in person.

Marty cackled, eyes bugged out, his hands clawing the air as I relayed the news. Tongue wagging, murderous Jack Nicholson in *The Shining* came to mind. With a taut smile, he asked no one in particular, one too many times, what fucking awful else the sons of bitches could tack on to the never-ending list. Frantic, I grasped at a threadbare silver lining to lure him out of this rage. He halted. Then brightened at the thought of all four of us going on our first family trip. In ten minutes our excitement was quashed when the travel agent quoted me the exorbitant four-ticket price tag. I wrote it on a sheet of paper. I could see in his despondent eyes the need to release the pent-up exasperation plaguing us both. At least the boys slept through this numbing scene.

On Sunday, we curtailed our family outing and bee-lined it to el Puente Principal, the congested main border crossing in Ciudad Juárez to attempt our next steps. An official, cleaning his fingernails with a letter opener, flat out told us it was illegal to obtain a FM-T (tourist visa) and a FM-3 (business visa) simultaneously. He asked for our passports as he glanced our way then returned to perfecting his nails. It set Marty off, craning his torso over the counter, sarcasm trumping his question. Our passports? This pissed off the burly official, who declared he could detect trouble in Marty's bloodshot eyes. I kicked Marty's shin. He glared at me. I glared back and pivoted my shins away from him, just in case. The phone rang. When the official turned away to answer, we argued in a seething whisper. By now we didn't care what Agustín and Ricardo did to the offices and lobbies, as long as they were within sight, we pretty much let them redecorate.

Another official, in civilian clothes, walked in and asked if we were being helped. We explained our predicament in a few concise sentences, like a finely tuned elevator pitch, but with only a touch of emotion or, we'd learned from past experience, they'd lose interest. He disappointed us by agreeing with his partner, but sympathized with the complexity of an international adoption and pushed his business card across the gleaming counter and proffered his assistance in renewing our tourist visas.

I eked out a thank you.

He shook his head, "We should be thanking you two."

We made plans to meet the next day, but as we walked, hand in hand, to the car, we agreed not to get too wrapped up in the official's promise. I again was grateful the boys didn't understand English.

The next day, he kept his word and we left with our updated visas. We took this as a good omen.

Twenty-four hours later, when Marty left for Baja California, my mission was to find the Registro Civil official who'd add the special annotation to Ricardo's birth certificate. On the second floor, in the maze of sweating, harried people, I ran into a familiar face. The statuesque lady who, in August, had given me her business card and said I'd found a friend for life took me by the hand and led us to the official's outer office. I hugged her. She nudged me through the door and blew the three of us a kiss. The secretary clued me in on how to approach Mr. Official so he'd sign Ricardo's birth certificate on the spot and not insist I return in a few days.

Mr. Official took one look at me, preened his hairline mustache, and went back to his work. Pompous jerk. I knew that reaction by heart. As soon as I greeted him in formal Spanish, without a gringa accent, he replaced the cap on his fountain pen, leaned forward, and looked directly at me. My mother would be proud. The boys seemed to comprehend the significance of this moment and sat still, hands in laps while the official, read each line front and back twice, cleared his throat like an opera diva while rolling his pen between thumb and index finger. Then with a dramatic flourish, his hand hovered in big circles until the pen touched down onto the designated line where he signed, stamped, and affixed the annotation. The three of us seemed to exhale in unison, making a hasty departure to the first floor where the photocopier had a long tail of a line.

We made copies, faxed one to María, and went straight back to the apartment. No way I'd miss Marty's call. I paced through dinner and didn't entertain Agustín's increasing demands to drop whatever we were doing and take him back to the orphanage. Wait for Papi to come back, we'll take you in the rental car, I bargained. My usual tried and true distractions—bubble gum, a sock puppet, videos—fell flat. Arms fastened across his chest, foot stomping, and veins protruding along his temples zapped my optimism. I braced myself. His conniption fit included flailing and writhing on the floor with intermittent shrieks, which scared the hell out of Ricardo and sent him into gushing tears. I ping ponged between reassuring my little one and preventing my eldest from hurting himself. Be patient, he's a wounded and confused four-year-old, I'd told myself, but

I harbored a dark desire to grant his wish and drive away from DIF with just Ricardo.

Who was this cold-blooded ruthless woman inside my body? If I met myself on the street, and confided these thoughts, I'd have nothing to do with me. I made the notoriously despicable La Llorona of Mexican mother folklore seem kind and rational. Prolonged prayer while doing the dishes and staring at the kitchen curtains brought a slight shift, enough to stop the anxious whirring from racing laps along my nervous system. In an attempt to balance out the day, despite my fatigue and doubts, I indulged them with art projects and let them smear watercolors on long sheets of paper, their clothes, the table, and floor, followed by cookies crushed into ice cream.

During these times, my oldest would shed his burden as head of household, a role forced upon him during his mother's long absences, and just be a little boy. But, like an unexpected icy drop of water plopping on his head, something would jerk Agustín out of his reverie and he'd storm over to me, shouting orders and badgering me with questions I had no answers for. When was his mother coming? Had I seen her pass by in her car and not tell him? He'd turn sullen, but Ricardo's persistent playfulness came to the rescue. This time a ribbon of toilet paper fluttered behind him like a kite as he ran in circles, drool flinging out both sides of his mouth. Once we're home, I surmised, Agustín will fall in love with Santa Cruz, our home, our life, and magically this longing will stop. Just hang on for a bit longer.

At 6:15 p.m. Marty called, his voice filled with relief and exhaustion. He'd arrived in the early afternoon at the Registro Civil office in pocket-sized Ciudad Constitución, a non-descript building resembling a house with three front doors. He opened the first one he came to, entering what looked like a typical lawyer's office with a desk, two chairs, and a bookcase along the back wall and hit pay dirt. In his most polite and assiduous Spanish, he presented our dilemma and requested the administrator behind the desk affix the annotation to Agustín's birth certificate. The robust but unpretentious woman posed a series of straightforward questions and then, much to Marty's relief, complied and placed the document back in his hands within minutes.

Almost immediately his sense of accomplishment was dashed. Instead of thanking her, he pointed out, with all due respect, the document differed from the one in Ciudad Juárez, and both certificates had to be identical to fulfill México City's requirements. He carefully proceeded to dispute the administrator when she insisted Baja California Sur's procedures and protocols differed from the northern country. The document would absolutely satisfy the capital's requirements. According to Marty, her body language and tone of voice, while not contentious or abrupt, signaled the end of their discussion.

Hours later when I imagined him robbed and left like road kill he called.

"I drove two hundred sixty kilometers back to La Paz in this shitty car, on shitty roads, and somehow found the DHL office before six. So I sent the certificate to María just in case something isn't one hundred percent correct. I'm not leaving until I hear from her."

The next day after conferencing with María, he sped off in the broiling heat back to Ciudad Constitución cursing our bad luck. His gut had been right. At least now she'd armed him with a faxed copy of Ricardo's annotated birth certificate, phone numbers of high-ranking officials in México City, and precise instructions, that if necessary, he could call María or one of the officials who could clarify our predicament.

This time he arrived late in the afternoon when the office had closed.

"I got a fucking flat tire half way through the trip and burned my hand on the lug wrench." He paused. For once, I didn't interject. "I cried like a baby."

Marty hung up to find a cold beer and a room for the night.

Before eight o'clock the next morning, he'd had come across a shop, he later told me, with a fax machine and planned out every step by the time he surprised the Registro Civil official as she stepped out of her car. He showed her Ricardo's birth certificate, clarified our request, and offered to pay for the phone calls to the capital where they'd confirm our special circumstances.

The protracted silence that ensued had my poor man squirming from the knots that were surely multiplying in his wrenching stomach. When she reached towards the bookshelf where a paltry set of school binders housed the town's law books and casually flipped from cover to cover, he envisaged a coin tossed high up in the air, falling in nauseating slow motion. Heads, we win. Tails, we lose.

She closed the binder and with a poker face proclaimed, "I do not see any law that authorizes me to make the inscription you require." Pause. He groaned, ready to pressure her into calling María, but in the next breath said, "But I also do not see any law that prevents me from doing so." He slumped into his chair, thanking her profusely as she affixed the inscription.

Once he faxed María the birth certificate, they spoke, he received a thumbs up, and she added how impressive it was he'd finagled the Superior Court Judge to perform the deed. Only then did he realize that the signature belonged to a high-level judge with the same last name as the boys. Small world? Freaky coincidence? Marty reasoned she'd had her chance to speak up if she was indeed a relative.

My knight in sweaty, dusty armor called me from La Paz after retracing his route to DHL.

"In the meantime, you need to fax María the most recent petition with the judges' signatures." My outdated, dog-eared copy was no longer valid.

I called Ms. D, who promptly said she'd meet us outside of family court first thing in the morning.

The night seemed eternal. I was acutely aware of needing a blanket most nights now. The heater was a blessing. It drowned out the sirens and never-ending sound of mufflerless traffic. Christmas. The thought of being here through the end of the year released a torrent of sobs. I bunched up the pillows to my face.

The next morning Ms. D led me and two groggy toddlers into the clerks' offices, where she spoke with an older gentleman yielding a huge pair of scissors and a much younger man holding a stack of petitions they were binding by hand with a gigantic sewing needle and thick thread. They looked like something out of a Grimm's fairytale. After a few minutes of polite conversation, she lowered her voice, paused, and nodded her response.

Then she led me back outside. The boys took off running like cartoon characters with spinning feet.

"Would you please, do me a favor and lend *me* four hundred pesos?"

I answered by counting out the amount as the boys circled back, skipping and laughing.

"Stay out here." Ms. D left without explaining. Upon her return, she invited me on a walk. For an instant, I thought she'd hook her arm in mine, lean against me, and whisper a confidence or a bit of gossip.

"It took two hundred fifty pesos for the head clerk to grant us permission and one hundred fifty to retrieve it from the basement archives." She tapped her watch and said, "We should return in half an hour for the copy."

I squeezed her arm. She remarked how content the boys seemed. Oh, if she'd only seen Agustín a few days ago spasming on the floor like he'd been demon possessed.

Thirty minutes later, the older gentleman handed me the crisp petition as we arrived at his counter. If I'd been allowed through the counters swinging doors, a group hug would've been in order, but instead the three of us gave a resounding thank you to the clerks, then we caught Ms. D off guard and hugged her. Regaining her composure, she introduced us to the clerks as another gentleman approached us. He was a dead ringer for George Stephanopoulos, and had approved the petition during the first and fourth round.

He took the time to elucidate our case. México City was still working out the kinks as we spoke. Ours was being used as the prototype for international adoption petitions. The first case to go through since the changes had become effective in July. He assured me that ours had been faster than most despite the additional requirements and cited cases that took years to complete. *Years?* The floor seemed to bottom out. Would I be trapped here like the fellow in Kafka's, *The Castle?*

Hours later, I was eleventh in line waiting for my turn at the fax machine. María needed an advance copy of the petition to ward off any possible glitches. Sweat trickled down my torso. The hands on the clock leapt forward. Time did not wait, didn't care if I had to arrange a pickup with DHL and get home to ready the packet before four. Less than two hours away. My patience wore thin as people in front of me fumbled with their documents or wallets. When a woman emptied her purse on the counter, every-one in line swore under their breath. The boys wanted to play hide and seek. Not now, I told them. They whimpered then whined like rusted machinery. Agustín pleaded in once sweet baby talk that weeks ago turned annoying, and now was abrasive. I threw him a death ray look. Ricardo threw himself on the floor. I shot him an arched don't-you-dare-look and didn't retrieve him up as the line shortened.

Somehow it all came together, relief flooding over me like a downed shot of tequila when the DHL guy tossed our package into the van and drove off.

The dark, soggy morning kept the boys asleep longer. Marty, who had by then returned from his adventure, cud-dled with me under a blanket on the sofa as we sipped our coffee.

"What are you thinking of?" Marty asked while hold-ing the mug in both hands.

"How grateful I'll be when I no longer have to move the sofa and table against the front door anymore." I looked over at Marty and saw his tears ahead of mine. We embraced in silence.

At eight thirty Marty couldn't stand the suspense and left to get an update on the boys' passports. I busied myself orchestrating the tiniest details, my heart racing, afraid Marty would throw open the door, face twisted, announcing we'd overlooked a step that required another rubber stamp, signature, or a few more days in Juárez. Any sound coming from outside brought hope and fear. When Marty returned, he was solemn. I held my gut in.

"The passports will be ready at—," he splayed two fingers in the air. I jumped into his arms.

"If all goes well, we'll be at the consulate tomorrow morning and have plenty of time to catch a plane home," Marty finished my thoughts.

An hour later we all went to DIF to say good-bye bearing gifts and flowers. When we told Agustín he could visit with his friends first, he chose not to after all. While his decision didn't surprise me, I deemed it as acceptance of family and life in Santa Cruz. Marty maneuvered us toward the front door. The director and Ms. D escorted us outside where we took photos and thanked each other over and over again before waving goodbye to the teary-eyed staff, who were thrilled to see the boys go. I couldn't look back.

By a quarter to two we were sitting in the stuffy passport lobby going through the INS packet to keep ourselves from wringing our hands in desperation. When we heard them call our name, I held my breath. No questions. No leafing through forms, only the sight of the boys' navy-blue passports and wishes for a safe trip home.

We hugged and kissed right in the middle of the parking lot, stopping traffic. No blast of car horns or yelling at us to move.

We drove through smog-laden, jam-packed streets saying good-bye to the parks, soccer stadium, restaurants, and mall where we'd found refuge and air-conditioning during the brutal summer months. I rolled down the window, exposing the tips of my fingers to the autumn breeze. My throat constricted. Was I truly going home? Not yet, whatever you do don't let your guard down, I scolded myself. Not until we're on the other side of this border, looking back at the coiled serpentine wire that topped the chain link fence. Keep your optimism in check, toes behind the yellow line, arms at your side, look straight ahead, and maybe the mythical tumblers in the universe will click, the gate will open, and you'll be free.

The boys beat us up the two flights of stairs to the INS office. One of the clerks was offering them a mint when we dropped our application onto the counter. Mr. W methodically looked over each document, called off its name, and flipped it into a new pile while Ms. X checked off the appropriate boxes on the copious list of requirements. I crossed my fingers, arms, and ankles. A series of signatures and stamps would promote us through the bureaucratic maze.

"So when can we pick up our packet?" Marty asked. "Tomorrow morning?"

"Not tomorrow morning. The investigator needs to go over the entire packet himself and may want to make some inquires." Ms. X packed away our file. "We were clear that this process could take anywhere from two to four weeks to complete."

"But we were under the impression that if we had every-thing in order, we'd be approved in twenty-four hours." Marty roared. Hands splayed on the counter. I fingered the hem on the backside of his T-shirt, as if rubbing a spark to detonate his rage. Go for it, I thought. Explode. I won't stop you. Not this time. Scare the shit out of these officious peo-ple who can go home each night to their families and life.

"You said it took longer when people *didn't* fol-low the in-struc-tions," he pounded the counter as he marched over to the end of the counter and back. "Didn't you just check off every box?"

"Yes, you did a fine job," Ms. X replied in a starched tone. "Now we need to do our job."

Marty, on tiptoes, arms and legs outstretched, seemed a tarantula poised to strike.

Mr. W bellied up to the counter. "We'll begin looking at it this afternoon. Call us in the morning."

"But don't expect to have your file approved tomorrow, understand?" Ms. X added as we herded the boys out the door. I suppressed the urge to flip her off.

Sleep eluded us. We brewed coffee before dawn.

Our breaths hung in the morning chill as the boys tossed pebbles in the INS parking lot long before the staff arrived. A few minutes after eight, the boys ran up the flight of stairs ahead of us.

"Yes. You heard right," Mr. W chuckled at our disbe-lief. Our packet had been approved. Like laboratory rats sprung out of a cage we dashed to the last hurdle.

After the heavily armed guards checked us for weap-ons, we filed into the boxy American Consulate building, where every square inch of space was covered in humans.

We found a corner where the boys reclined against our bodies. I zeroed in on the doors, wondering which one would open, and who would announce another oversight, causing us to start over like a Monopoly game: Do not pass go. Do not collect the boys' visas. Go to adoption limbo.

Marty's calculated pessimism suggested we should just resign ourselves that one or more surprises could screw up the entire day. I slipped my arm through his, girding myself for the worst. When a door flung open revealing a dour-looking woman in a chartreuse pantsuit, my nerve endings prickled, shooting static from head to toe, leaving me nauseated. Our name wasn't called. Breathe, I told myself. Breathe, say a Hail Mary, and breathe.

Our name rung out like the Liberty Bell. I flung Ricardo under my arm like a sack of potatoes and sprinted to our numbered station.

We approached a thick bulletproof window where a woman spread our paperwork in front of her. A brief introduction led to a multitude of questions in a tedious monotone until Ms. Y, hair gilded in hairspray, pushed our packet through the opening.

"Now go to the medical clinic next door and get the boys medical examinations. They will send us the results. Come back at three for your visas."

Like an assembly line a steady stream of people filed out of one building into another where within minutes we met a young doctor who asked me to undress Agustín then Ricardo. I was curious to see what her opinion was of the boys' health, but it took me longer to undress and dress the boys than the exam did. She asked three medically irrelevant questions, glanced at the boys, and sent us on our way with the signed medical forms after recommending circumcision for both of them.

"Did she say circumcision?" I asked as the door closed behind her. Marty rolled his eyes.

We went back to the apartment, picked up our luggage and rental deposit, and said our good-byes to Manuel and the neighbors, who escorted us to the car.

Manuel blessed Agustín and Ricardo on the forehead with his index finger and thumb forming a cross. His chin quivered as he enveloped them in his big burly arms and told them to be good. He shook Marty's hand and told him to take care of us all. Then he blessed me with one hand while wiping his eyes with the other.

I threw my arms around him. "Thank you so very much."

His chest tightened and heaved as we embraced.

One of the neighbors said, "He's crying because he's going to miss your desserts."

The laughter eased the sadness. They followed the car as we rounded the corner, waving and wishing us a bounty of good luck until we disappeared into traffic. Good-bye pay phone, corner market, stationary store, Sanborn's, and fear.

A bit after three o'clock we stood in front of Ms. Y where she pushed the boys' visas through the slot toward us. "Enjoy your children. I'm expecting another one of my own in six months."

We congratulated her.

"Now proceed to the border crossing and stop at customs for their exit interview." She grinned. Our mouths dropped open.

"Border interview?" I looked at Marty.

"No one ever told us about a border interview." Marty said.

"I'm sorry, but you must stop at the border, go to main lobby, and present your documents." She smiled, folded her hands, and looked beyond us. There was a room full of people wanting to be in our place.

"Hey, at least we're heading in the right direction." Marty forced a smile as we stepped through the metal detectors.

Once the rush hour traffic slowed down to a crawl, the border crossing came into view. We inched our way up to the crest of the asphalt bridge where we caught sight of the string of booths, each of which housed a computer loaded with information about every vehicle and driver's license, ready to snatch a drug trafficker, rapist, kidnapper, thief, or arms dealer. The boys were asleep, heads back, mouths open. They were troopers. Especially during the last few days when I commandeered them from one task to another forsaking play time. Self-reproach encumbered my thoughts. Santa Cruz would soften my rough edges, obscure my doubts, and gift me with a fairy godmother disposition.

"Well, here you are crossing the border back into the States. I don't see you kissing the asphalt," Marty chuckled and retrieved me from my ruminations.

The traffic had stopped, drivers cut their engines, and passengers stretched their legs as hawkers and beggars made their rounds to accordion-heavy *narco-traficante* music. I got out of the car and took in both countries simultaneously, as I had as a child growing up in my beloved *ambos* Nogales, where two countries seemed like one. My emotions swelled as I went down on my knees, tears streaming down my face as I kissed the ground. I stood up and met Marty's watery eyes. He reached for my hand. I clasped it. Team Santa Cruz would prevail.

A half-hour later Marty veered over into the furthest right-hand lane away from the border crossing itself and steered the car toward the stark concrete buildings and adjacent parking lot.

"It might be better for us to crash in El Paso, have a good dinner, and sleep before we go home."

"You don't think we'll make the last flight out?" I rubbed the boys' warm thighs to wake them up.

My husband shook his head.

The cavernous, air-conditioned lobby sported a wall-to-wall counter, separating the officials' domain from the citizens. Our side had rows of uncomfortable plastic seats where you took a paper number and waited.

"We're in luck, the place seems to be clearing out." Marty surveyed the room.

The boys and I were looking out the windows counting red and blue cars when they called our name.

Mr. Z, a fireplug of a man, shook our hands and welcomed us back home with a patter of small talk as he perused our documents. The boys were fidgeting, curious about every little thing on the counter, and Agustín kept asking when we were going to eat. I'd run out of crackers, water, candy, fruit, and gave him the backpack and told him to look for himself.

Our interviewer, a sweet man, doled out compliments and bumper sticker platitudes as he got our documents in order, but I was fried, deep-fried, and wanted him to shut up.

Yeah, yeah, just please, do your job. My lips were sealed, but my eyes bugged out. We have a plane to catch, a life waiting for us!

He retreated behind the partition like the Wizard of Oz while I frenetically paced the length of the building and the boys zigzagged after me like ducklings.

Marty called out, gesturing us to get back.

Mr. Z handed us our documents and said, "Mr. and Ms. Picco, have a safe trip and may God bless you all."

We bolted to the car. I rolled down the window and yelled out that I was home as we crossed the border and left Juárez behind in the smog. Agustín molded a bright yellow piece of Play-Doh. Ricardo chewed on his. I extended my hand to him and felt the wet blob hit my palm.

"Can we please make the last flight?" I pleaded.

"I'm going to try, babe. Hang on." Marty navigated through El Paso rush hour traffic like a New York cabbie toward the airport. I dialed the airline's number as soon as Marty's cell phone had service.

"If it's meant to be, Liz, there'll be seats on this flight; if not, we'll leave on the first flight out in the morning. Okay?"

I nodded, but it wasn't okay. I prayed to wring out one last favor from the gods. I promised they wouldn't hear from me for a while, I'd place a moratorium on my pleas, if only they'd grant this final one.

"There are plenty of seats, but the flight leaves in less than an hour."

"No problem," Marty said as he made a right turn onto an empty street. Every light turned green and stayed green as we crossed each intersection. No one preceded us at the rental car counter. The boys didn't have to go to the bathroom and a porter took our bags and checked them in, so we reached our gate with time left to call our mothers.

"I'm in El Paso, Mom." I squeaked out the good news.

"¡Gracias a Dios!" My mother and I wept, then laughed with joy.

Agustín and Ricardo clung to our legs, peering up at us with worried smiles.

I boarded the plane with a tremendous sense of accomplishment, but no relief. The familiar anxiety crept up. I feigned excitement, hoping Marty wouldn't notice my clammy hands, parched mouth, and overwhelming impatience as the plane filled up in dribbles. Sit down. Buckle up. Close the door. Pull back. Taxi us out of here. Now. I barked orders to passengers, stewardesses, and the pilots, I never said out loud. Fear pulsated through my body, afraid a mustached official from DIF, INS, SRE, or the Consulate would materialize and demand one more thing from us. We'd be handcuffed in order to comply and watch the plane taxi down the tarmac without us.

I reached for Marty's hand for reassurance. He was enthusiastically explaining the airplane features to the boys and I didn't have the heart to interrupt them. They were both enthralled by the headphones spilling out music, the little upright tables with the special place for their drink, and the window covering Agustín was lowering and raising. The plane taxied down the runway to the boys squealing with delight.

CHAPTER XIX

HOMECOMING 1998

Marty sped down Highway 17's summit, taking blind curves through the Santa Cruz Mountains with an unnerving nonchalance. Black tire marks and gouges marred the inside surface of the concrete median, a gruesome, yet overlooked, reminder that accidents and gnarled traffic were a routine occurrence for impatient commuters and unsuspecting tourists. I braced my feet against the floor mats, my hands clamped on the edges of the car seat while I eagle-eyed the lanes up ahead for a stalled car hugging the meager shoulder or deer bolting out of the dense evergreen. Marty seemed oblivious I'd spent the last five months as a flat-lander, and it didn't help matters the boys whooped it up at every curve encouraging their enthusiastic father to go faster. I figured it must be the testosterone and kept quiet, not wanting to start an argument on our first day home. Once we passed the Glen Canyon and Vine Hill exits, the highway straightened out and the canopy of green fell away affording us a view. I pointed to the shimmering ocean in the distance.

"That's Santa Cruz. Our home." The swath of city lights below us made for a Peter Pan moment. Hoarse with emotion, I reached into the backseat, caressed the boy's soft legs as Highway 17 ended and moments later we exited towards the coast.

Familiar landmarks, our bank, favorite breakfast hangouts, and funky secondhand shops butted up against boxy commercial construction as we neared our neighborhood. Marty drove along the coast and rolled down the windows, pointing to the ocean lit up by the moon and streetlamps. Salty fresh air replaced the stench of traffic fumes. The boys strained to lift and tip themselves from their car seats to survey the wide swath of glistening water. Marty decelerated while we rubbernecked until he spotted headlights in the rearview mirror.

"Does it have a deep end like the pool?" Agustín asked.

We laughed and said "Yes, but it's much colder than the pool." I promised we'd explore tomorrow.

I studied the curvy street dotted with Monterey cypress pines, the silhouettes of the branches seeming to jack-knife over the cliffs. I frowned, noticing quirky, quaint beach cottages had been demolished and were being transformed into expansive, two-story homes. Fortunately our favorite corner store remained intact, as I'd last seen it, down to the poster-laden windows with beanie-capped kids skateboarding just shy of the front door. I wiped my eyes as Marty turned down our street a block from the ocean cliffs. As he pulled into the driveway, he pressed his rolled-up hand to his lips and sounded a trumpet to announce our modest ranch-style home. The porch light glowed like a golden beacon.

"*La casa americana.*" Agustín shouted.

We piled out of the car and stood on our postcard-sized lawn savoring the fragrance and sounds of the waves. No unrelenting sirens. Some of our neighbors' lights were on, TVs flickered behind blinds, and couples strolled by hand in hand towards the beach while bicycles flashed by in the distance. Cars uniformly inched up next to fences and lawns on both sides of the pot-holed street. When Marty activated the garage door Ricardo cowered as the metal door groaned and disappeared overhead. Agustín, undeterred as usual, raced through the garage straight to the kitchen door, turning the knob with a vengeance, but it wouldn't cooperate. Once Marty unlocked the door and turned on the light, our oldest took deliberate steps through the kitchen, opening the lower drawers and cupboards and surveying the counters.

"What's that?" He pointed to the toaster and seemed mesmerized that bread disappeared into the machine and then popped up brown and warm. When he couldn't open the much bigger refrigerator door, the alphabet magnets caught his attention. I spelled out his name. He turned the *G* and *T* upside down. A droopy-eyed Ricardo was still at the door, glommed onto the back of Marty's leg, showing little interest. Would it last or would we have to install those pesky baby lock gadgets? When Agustín passed through the small dining room into the living room, we nudged Ricardo forward. Our eldest stood in front of the sofa, hands on hips, puzzled by the fireplace, but instantly drawn to the poker and bellows.

"I'm a pirate."

"That's not a toy," we said in unison, while Marty helped him put the poker back on its stand. He patted the sofa, beckoning Ricardo to join him as he sat and bounced. His little brother filled the space between Marty's legs and refused. I compiled an inventory of sharp edges, lamp cords, and tall bookcases. When Marty pointed the way to their bedroom and toys, Agustín barreled down the hallway. As Ricardo lagged behind, we could hear Agustín's gasps as he entered their bedroom. When we reached the bedroom door, he was stroking the Bugs Bunny quilts and stuffed animals piled on the pillows.

"Look, Licalo."

Ricardo shot a look at his crib and dove for a rubber ball instead while Agustín opened books, tested the Tonka dump truck, and pounded on a Tom Tom. I slumped down against the doorjamb and watched them as my heart somersaulted. Soon after Agustín spied the bike and trike parked in a corner and fondled the streamers on the handlebars. When Marty plopped our oldest onto the bike seat, he looked pained, but smiled. Was he afraid we'd take it away? Ricardo chased after the ball down the hallway into the bathroom. He inspected every inch of the toilet and flushed it with glee.

"Oh, no," I groaned, reminding him it wasn't a toy. I pulled out the stool so Ricardo could reach the faucets and wash his hands. They made faces in the mirror and our little one giggled, showing off his Jack o' lantern smile. Agustín played with the bathtub toys as I wandered into our bedroom to find a new bed, rustic distressed pine, like in my dreams.

Marty wrapped me in his arms, nuzzled his face into my hair, and said, "Welcome home." My vision blurred as I slipped off my shoes and jumped onto the bed. We spooned. Marty tossed his side of the fluffy comforter over us. The sounds of the boys' discoveries, Ricardo's two-word questions, and Agustín's authoritative answers brought contented smiles.

When the boys galloped into our room, we pulled back the comforter, patted the bed, and Marty yelled, "Family burrito."

Agustín leapt in between us and Ricardo snuggled up against my body. Was there anything better than the warm knot of arms and legs? We were home. The luxurious comfort of home and fatigue bore down on my eyelids, but I was afraid to close my eyes. What if this was a dream?

After tucking the boys in several times, we toasted with a glass of wine and watched them sleep, arm in arm, before heading to bed.

The next morning, I awoke startled, expecting bright sunlight to outline the water stain marks on the ceiling of my bedroom in Suites Victoria. Instead fog softened the morning light. I loosened my clenched limbs. Marty snored in a deep sleep. I perked my ears for a sound emanating from our sons' room, down the hallway. Satisfied the morning was still mine, I reacquainted myself with our bedroom and didn't reach for my journal. No need to cross out another day on my makeshift calendar.

Life in Juárez was over.

One hundred and twenty-seven days. Almost three times the length of stay I'd rashly projected in that rats' nest of a city. I wondered if I had to do it over again, would I? When I thought of the boys the answer seemed obvious, but when selfishness crept in I wasn't so sure.

Overnight life became simpler. Marty was minutes away at work. I had a car, a computer, and, best of all, the living room furniture stayed in its place at night.

The next morning, the sudden ringing of the phone startled us while the boys finished brushing their teeth. The answering machine clicked on as they bolted into the dining room. The boys gaped at the little black gadget when it played our greeting. Faces scrunched up, they hovered over the machine, but jumped back when the beep sounded. Ricardo peeked from behind me, eyeing the contraption. Agustín inspected the plastic box as our neighbor's voice welcomed us home and offered their help. I translated.

"You see, Licalo, the American house is full of magic," Agustín said.

We cocooned like new parents bringing home their babies from the hospital. Ricardo was leery of everything, running under his bed at the sound of the garbage disposal or vacuum cleaner. The perforation in his eardrum exacerbated loud noises at close range, but he couldn't tolerate earplugs or cotton balls, so instead I learned to give him a heads up.

By the third day my four-year-old delegated certain chores to Ricardo and reprimanded me for changing our Juárez routine. When I'd explain, he'd curl his hand around his chin and argue until he got his way. A born leader, negotiator, or pain in the ass?

Mornings after breakfast I'd pull the boys in their Radio Flyer wagon to the library or stroll the beach close to the rocks where the boys felt safe from the waves. The first day when they'd dug their toes into the sand, near the water's edge and gawked at an intimidating winter swell, they tore their hands from mine, mute with fear, and fled from the monstrous waves. When I collected and comforted them, they shivered, faces ashen, begging to go back to the house.

"Accidente," Agustín wailed. The front of his jeans were soaking wet. Ricardo's diaper had probably kept his pants dry, but drool squirted out both sides of his mouth like a Saint Bernard eyeing a steak.

"I'm so, so sorry. It's Mami's fault." I scooped them up, kissed their soggy faces, and retreated. How could I be so dense? Later Marty laughed and dismissed my paranoia that I'd traumatized them for life.

Afternoons were filled with lunch, naps, and tree climbing or parading their bikes around the backyard. When they slipped and fell down, from a low branch, then stood up unharmed and splotched in mud, I applauded.

"You're supposed to get dirty," I chuckled. Their sheepish, puzzled looks turned victorious while I recounted childhood stories. "When I was your age, my brothers and sisters and I would go out after a summer rain just to make mud. We'd find the biggest puddles like this one and mix it up with sticks." Agustín ran off and came back with my garden spade and trowel, I'd left by the garden hose.

"Perfect. Now stir until it's thick and gloppy." Mud splattered on their rain boots and jeans.

"Like this." Agustín cupped a thick blob of mud.

"Yep. Then we'd look for twigs and dried leaves to mix in the mud." I led them through the yard, collecting bits of leaves and dried grass.

Ricardo molded a series of balls and Agustín made pies as I shaped bricks.

"Your uncles and aunts and I would make mud bricks to build a small fort." I led them to the sunny walkway where we placed our wares to dry. After a few hours, the boys preferred to smash theirs against the back fence delighting in the spray of dirt clods.

On the fourth day while baking cookies, the boys smeared oatmeal raisin dough on their fingers and licked with approval. As soon as the first batch disappeared into the oven, Agustín stepped off the stool.

"Where's my suitcase?"

"But the cookies aren't ready." I teetered. "We'll visit Juárez when you get your American passport, but this is home now."

His forlorn and panicked look alarmed me. I cradled him, in part, to safeguard him from my crestfallen reaction. Ricardo stroked his brother's heart. I wiped his tears. In between hiccups, he cried out for his mother and the orphanage.

I'd anticipated crossing the threshold into the United States would be akin to entering Disneyland through Snow White's castle into the happiest place on earth. I'd banked on the enchantment of a home brimming with toys, treats, and family love to help him release the past. Truth be told, I was certain the allure of American life would soon blur what he'd left behind. My naïveté was boundless.

The multicolored suitcase with wheels and long red handle came out of the closet. Agustín packed while Ricardo and

I finished baking the cookies. Not long after he parked the suitcase by the door. I placed milk and cookies on the table and made a big show of savoring each mouthful. I helped Ricardo onto his booster seat. Agustín inched over to the table. I pretended not to notice and when his hand reached for the first cookie, I left them there and escaped to the bedroom.

"This is awful," I whimpered to Marty on the phone. "Nothing's changed."

"Take a deep breath. Call Georgia." Marty's impatience amped my feelings of incompetence. I didn't recognize that I'd just caught him at a shitty time when office politics were in high gear.

I called the social worker that'd conducted our home study a year earlier and had adopted five children from all over the world. She empathized, but advised me to chill out. Embarrassed, I listened as she reiterated this behavior was common in older children like Agustín who'd been left in institutions for long periods of time.

"But he's so loved," I persisted.

"Love isn't enough."

I wanted to reach through the phone and slap her.

"Trust me, I know. Give him time and structure."

My sons stood at my doorway, grinning, cookie crumbs and milk bubbles covered their mouths and chins. My time was up.

The quiet homecoming vanished by the end of the week when, after a nap, the doorbell and knocking rattled us awake. Ricardo began to cry at the loud noises echoing through the house. Agustín raced through the hallway.

"Stop, mijito. Wait. Don't open the door." His disturbing Juárez habit of running to strangers and not waiting for permission would be hard to break. I smoothed out my clothes, raked my fingers through my hair, and then swooped Ricardo up.

"It's your neighbors." I stiffened at the booming sound of voices.

"Just a minute."

Agustín pawed at the doorknob in anticipation while Ricardo plunged his chubby face into my chest and hung on like a Koala bear to bamboo.

I opened the door, voices escalated, neighbors I hadn't seen in several months threw their arms around Agustín and me, engulfing us both. Camera flashes blinded us as a flood of neighbors poured into our small living room. Rose, Sam, and their three teenage boys were first in line, then Harriet, Gus, their bickering adolescent daughter and son, plus the retired couple down the street, and Sharon whose English rose garden was the talk of the neighborhood.

"Hola."

"Oh they're beautiful, Liz."

"What a blessing."

"Now, how do you pronounce his name?"

"I like Tino instead." The teenage boys swung Agustín into the air.

"Yes, let's call him Tino."

"Do you have any sodas for our boys?" Our neighbors asked as they ushered their kids into the dining room. "They just came back from skateboarding."

"How about Rico for Ricardo?"

I bristled at the nicknames. So did Agustín, who kept repeating his name when they called him Tino. The teenagers roughhoused and passed him from one to the other. He lapped it up while Ricardo refused to greet anyone and choked me with his death grip. I answered simultaneous questions then held up my free hand to translate for Agustín and give the crowd his answer. I maneuvered Ricardo onto my lap, the only space left in the living room, and adjusted my mangled clothes. Just when my little one relaxed enough to face one of the neighbor's playful fingers the phone rang. He wailed. It was Marty. In whispered tones, I begged him to come home.

"We've been invaded." I half laughed, half whimpered.

"Oh no. I told them to wait until the weekend," Marty groaned.

"I feel guilty complaining. They mean well, but it's overwhelming."

"They're just excited for us."

I informed the lively group that Ricardo wasn't feeling well. He was sobbing now and burrowed deeper into my chest.

"I'm going to give him a bath. Thank you so much for stopping by." I waved away offers to help bathe the boys and asked Agustín to take people's hands and lead them out the door. He shook everyone's hand and asked them to come back soon as he bid them good-bye. When the last set of shoes crossed the door, I closed and locked it, sighing with relief. I spied the suitcase. Thank goodness not one of them mentioned it propped against the living room wall. We ran back to bed where I read to them and waited for Marty to come home.

Marty was eager to show his family off, but he listened to his older brothers' and sisters' wisdom on these matters and respected my wishes. A laser-fine divide emerged between us without an argument or accusations to define it. Our time together sifted into the boys' needs and wants, our relationship obscured by the towering mound of priorities.

The first Sunday home the boys accompanied Marty to his soccer game and left me alone. Savoring the Indian summer afternoon on the back deck, eyes closed to drift into the hypnotic sound of the surf. My limp body sank into the padded chair, my breathing quieted, and I inventoried the simple, ordinary things I'd no longer take for granted. Solitude. Spontaneity. Cussing. Making love. Sleeping through the night. Privacy.

My chest welled up. Face contorted. Deep guttural wails jerked and bucked my body. What the hell? Stop this, I demanded. Count your blessings. Remember Oprah's commandments: take deep breaths, make a gratitude list, and be present. But not even Ms. Winfrey could dyke the deluge of tears. This wasn't a torrent of relief or crescendo of joy. I didn't know what the tears were for. I went into the house for the box of tissues. Did it matter? Just cry and go on to the next thing, because no way would I complain. What would Marty say? What would anyone say? I couldn't complain, not now, not after begging to be a mother.

I zipped my discontent into an enormous mental beanbag and stashed it in a corner. Meanwhile I'd concentrate on day care, pediatricians, and my Web design business.

The following week Ricardo still woke up crying with each new noise—rain spilling into gutters, garage doors opening and closing, skateboards butting up to curbs, the foghorn's moan. Poor baby. I whispered in his ear to clutch his panda, roll over, and go back to sleep. He did. Thankfully, Agustín slept through everything. I stood over each bed and watched them. I remembered opening my eyes from a deep sleep as a child and seeing the outline of a familiar figure in our bedroom doorway and feeling safe at the sight of my mother. Had my mother felt like I did: afraid, raw, and unsure? Would I have the courage to ask her? Did I want to hear her answer? Afraid the comparison would set us apart even more, I shuttered my feelings. Suck it up, I scolded myself. You sound like an ungrateful malcontent.

October 27th

Went to work while Marty worked at home and stayed with the kids. I arrived early and felt nostalgic to be back in the office I had thought of longingly for five months. I felt removed from the fray and for once insecure even though I was so glad to be back. I felt better once I tidied up my desk and space, checked my e-mail and made some phone calls. I am slowly getting back into the swing of what used to be my life. One thing is for sure—I will not be able to work full-time any longer. Wow, I can't believe I just wrote that.

October 30th

Preschool was rough on Ricardo and me. He cried, and it broke my heart to see him run after me when the staff suggested I leave. I didn't. He

*clung to me whimpering while we sat in a corner
while the rest of the group played a game on the
rug and then listened to a story. I left when they
went outside to play and Ricardo was clamber-
ing up the slide without looking around for me.
Agustín sat back on the director's lap, waving
good-bye.*

When I picked up the boys, a flyer announcing the next
day's Halloween party was shoved into my hand. The guilt
tanked me. Icy numbing panic followed. On the way to
the car I remembered my mother hauling a faded old sheet
over me, measuring two eyeholes and sending me out the
door with a pillowcase in hand, but I couldn't do that to
the boys. Not on their first Halloween. By the time we got
to the store, the costumes were severely picked over. At our
second stop, two decimated aisles of Halloween products
held several piles of mismatched costumes where I pieced
together a complete Winnie-the-Pooh costume for Agustín
and Dalmatian for Ricardo.

Once at home, we practiced trick or treating at the door
with their Halloween bags.

Late in the afternoon the doorbell announced a steady
stream of monsters, fairies, and ghosts wanting candy.
Agustín's hearty laughter filled the house as he gave out
candy. Ricardo ran in horror.

At dusk Marty led the boys down the street with a passel of neighbors trailing behind photographing the blessed
event. I stayed home giving out candy. When they returned
an hour later, with sticky faces and hands, Ricardo and
Agustín dumped their booty on the table, marveling at the

pile of shiny wrapped chocolates, bubble gum, glittery pencils, taffy, glow-in-the-dark stickers, and bags of cookies. Would they ever fall asleep?

The next morning I found Agustín in his Halloween costume, ready to do it again. We'd forgotten to tell him that Halloween was only once a year.

CHAPTER XX

NOVEMBER 1998

November 6th

I have been stalking them with my camera taking candid photos of them while they explore their backyard. I have recorded their efforts at climbing trees in pursuit of hummingbirds and butterflies, laying on the ground head to head captivated by earthworms and snails, making designs on the ground as they peed when they thought no one was watching and playing with an abandon and delight that I treasure.

Agustín entertained us at dinnertime with bits of songs and phrases in English he'd learned in pre-school, but I reveled that Spanish, my first language, reigned in our household as it did in my mother's home.

"¿Sabes, Mami que leche es 'muh-elk' en Inglés?" He tumbled out the syllables for milk then pointed to his plate, glass, and fork, translating each from Spanish into English, beaming with pride. That moment swiped up a decades' old memory of my mother swaggering into the kitchen one weekend while her brood polished off breakfast. She gestured with a rolled up *Reader's Digest* in one hand for us to pipe down and poured herself an umpteenth cup of coffee with the other. A Mexican-bred debutante, sans high school diploma, she delighted in stumping her college-bound kids with newly acquired English vocabulary from the monthly *Word Power* section. Standing center stage in front of the stove, she scowled like Marlon Brando then addressed us across the counter as we scarfed down our chorizo con huevos and gulped milk.

"I'm horny!" she yelped. "Hor-nee, hor-nee, hor-nee." Punctuating each syllable with the *Reader's Digest* like a conductor's baton.

Food and drink sprayed in every direction. Our round of side-splitting laughter stymied my mother.

"¡Mamá!" My brothers pretended horror while one of my younger sisters, still in elementary school, blanched and pushed her plate away.

"Well, I am," she peristed and pointed to the bolded word as I read the entry.

"Ornery, Mom. You're ornery."

"That's what I said, horny."

A few weeks later, after cheering Marty's soccer team from the sidelines and mingling with the players at half time, Agustín added, "hot damn" and "those fuckers" to his expanding English catalogue.

Ricardo on the other hand mixed his own brand of Spanish with bits of English, so deciphering his utterances became a game of charades, particularly when there wasn't an object he could point to. We'd call out the wrong words in a frenzy to solve his mysterious vocabulary and, more than once, hurt his feelings by laughing at our crazy attempts. His frustration escalated after restating the words, one too many times, until he'd flop his shaking head onto his hands and dissolve into tears. Then to add insult to injury, Agustín, his trusty decoder, started shrugging his shoulders and telling his little brother he couldn't understand him either. It took a while before we culled some patterns: he replaced the *S* or *Sh* sound with a *T* or *K*, depending on the word. Aha! Howt was house and tooki wasn't turkey, but sushi.

As much as I loved having a family, I couldn't shake a nagging sense of a misstep. Nightmares and anxiety mushroomed, especially after joining a younger mothers' playgroup. Some of these sweet, perky women wore matching adult/child outfits and traded tales of parenting nirvana as they swapped hand-picked, homemade berry roll ups and almond milk smoothies from color-coordinated containers. Our foil-wrapped homemade bean and Mexican cheese burritos, dug out of a plastic mercado bag, were politely declined even though I reiterated that, unlike my mother, I didn't cook with lard. My heart went out to the salivating toddlers lurking to snatch the pint-sized cartons of Safeway chocolate milk from the boys. One week we brought extras for twin boys who circled us like vultures as soon as we dipped our hands into the bag. While their mother was occupied correcting the ingredients for a macrobiotic muffin recipe, they ripped open the milk cartons and chugged like truck drivers downing a cold one. The four boys were patting their stomachs and belching when the twins' mom using her 'outside voice' demanded like a vice cop they put their cartons down. Now! Didn't I know the wax on the carton could be toxic? I apologized, feigning disbelief as she replaced the childhood elixir with vanilla soy in a sippy cup.

When I complained about the tote bags under my eyes from sleep deprivation or bemoaned my glitter-splotched, ruined favorite sweater, the group of dew-eyed females cocked their heads, moved side to side in unison, and recited what seemed like a prose poem about these being part of our miraculous mothers' medals. When they praised their kid for eating mineral-rich boogers or applauded a budding self-esteem after a kid slapped them and called them names, I restrained myself. I wouldn't have spanked them or hurled a banana at the back of their heads, but I'd explain and correct gross and rude behavior. Soon after, I pulled the ejection handle.

I confided my doubts and regrets to no one, not my best friend, not my mother-in-law, not Marty, not even my therapist—and I paid her. Once or twice, I stuck my foot into the psychotherapy pond, testing her reaction, but backed out when I worried she saw Mommy Dearest sitting opposite her. Instead, I yelled my regrets out to high tides as waves crashed against the rocks, scrawled complaints on wet sand with driftwood, but was disappointed when the thin layer of bone chilling water didn't erase the doubts along with my words.

Fortunately, there were periods of contentment and overwhelming love towards the boys that fostered a robust scaffold I could grasp and build upon. I convinced myself that the solution was to be Super Madre, minus the cape and bustier, juggling home, children, marriage, and my business. Multi-tasking from one hour to the next, passing the boys off to Marty when he wasn't buried in keeping his business afloat. Agustín and Ricardo, given their past, understandably were suspicious of day care and agonized if we were a minute or two late. What started out as a manageable four hours a day, three times a week schedule was soon whittled down to three hours, twice a week, and some days Ricardo's mounting anxiety prompted a call from the staff for an early pick up. I had no choice, but take them to my overcrowded office where my childless co-workers and college interns, bless their hearts, welcomed them without reproach. Having our offices located on the same floor in a complex where a cookie company baked and shipped their goods made our lives more feasible. A built-in fragrantly sweet bribe kept the boys from interrupting us, most of the time, as we worked. We'd picnic outside on grassy patches then I'd put them down for a nap on portable floor mats. Agustín stretched out under my desk reading a book while Ricardo curled up beneath the credenza, clasping and sucking on my ankle as he fell sleep. My productivity suffered, though, clients grumbled, and I toyed with the idea of mainlining caffeine to keep all the balls in the air.

The first casualty was the marriage ball. Marty came home religiously for dinner and spent time with the boys, but returned to the office long after I'd fallen asleep. On weekends, we caught up on household chores and took shifts clocking in more hours at work to keep failure at bay. Baby sitters were out of the question; even our seasoned neighborhood parents who gladly offered to give us a childless couple of hours struck out. It seemed the boys knew just when we'd settled into a sumptuous booth to spend time alone. Marty's cell phone would ring. Our neighbors apologized profusely. We'd down our drink and head home.

We had the good luck of still lusting for each other, but we'd fall asleep during foreplay and in the morning, when we'd previously enjoyed playful lovemaking, we'd stir to find the boys camping out on our bed. On top of that, the unattractiveness of my short fuse did little to heighten our intimacy. It was no fun to take on the role of Wicked Witch to Marty's affable Goofy, and we endured frosty days with little contact. But we loved each other and we kept both feet in our marriage. Plus, we'd made a pact. Once we had a family – a deal was a deal.

When the business ball faltered, I'd scramble to pick it up, and kept it in the air, but for shorter periods of time. My once agile, quick brain wasn't soldiering along. I'd find myself scribbling a grocery list during meetings, made costly mistakes when drafting proposals, and frustrated my overextended colleagues, who were fielding an overload of clients. Marty was supportive and rallied to help, but I kept losing traction. My balancing act cratered when interns received offers for bona fide employment and one of my co-workers gave me her notice. It was her due to follow her passion into the world of journalism. By that point, I lacked the energy to train new interns and find a suitable replacement for my talented colleague. I relented and pulled the plug on my business. I delivered on my contracts to established clients, plus found them each a new agency to work with, and took three month to close up shop. I consoled myself, I'd have time to write and be with the boys.

Soon after, I stripped myself of Super Madre status when the relentless question of *what if* reared its ugly, pimply head. I'd wake up in the middle of the night like I'd been spring-loaded from a sound sleep. I'd sit up scared to death with my heart pounding and mouth so dry I couldn't make a sound. What the fuck was wrong with me? I asked for motherhood. No—I nagged and badgered. This hadn't been an accident.

"What is it?" Marty would stir.

"I don't know."

He sat up next to me.

I cried. Marty held me in the dark until I was spent.

"I'll go check on the boys." I'd insist Marty go back to sleep. "I'm fine."

I'd walk around the house parting curtains and looking out windows, and then I'd check in on the boys, whose profiles were illuminated by their night-lights. I'd brush the hair away from their foreheads and kiss their plump cheeks. Standing at their doorway, I recalled a panel of guest speakers at an adoption agency, years ago, parents who'd adopted, gushing about the instant they'd held their child a warm butterscotch sensation flowed through their veins and a bulletproof bond was born. But they didn't touch upon how that bond could weaken at times. To rattle me even worse, the possible boomerang effect of what goes around, comes around terrorized me. If I was capable of feeling like this, then my sons could and would feel the same way about me. This wasn't supposed to happen. What if these rancid emotions didn't fade away?

After two rainy and foggy seasons of intense thrashing and no change in sight, I confided in a wise older friend.

"It's those old Kodak moments of yours, Liz." She took my hand in hers.

"Take each one out of its protective sleeve, put it under an objective light, and examine it thoroughly. Only then," she advised, "will you see each expectation for what it truly is? And maybe, you'll stop these comparisons."

I looked deep into her eyes and thought, "Yeah, right. Whatever."

In time, I followed my wise friend's advice and revisited a journal from Ciudad Juárez. Maybe it was time for me to confront my fears and write about my less-than-perfect journey to motherhood. At first, I opened then slammed shut each one of the four notebooks I'd kept, afraid the entries would somehow find themselves on the front page of our newspaper and brand me for life. Then I acquiesced and read where I'd spewed out my desperation over my *what if's* for seven consecutive pages. There were sweet moments I'd managed to somehow record and caustic ones where I thought I'd totally screwed up. I shuddered at my fear and marveled how the boys had thrived despite starting off in a city that seemed to be devouring its own decent, hard-working people. In rereading the first months of my entries, I'd assumed in a year or so I would know more, have answers, and possibly shed my expectations and settle into my new skin. Not so, but I'd made a slight shift.

Our first anniversary together, the boys and I baked a cake and strung streamers in the dining room. This time while the cake rose in the oven, the suitcase stayed in the closet. The boys showed off more of their English, but like my mother, I insisted we speak in Spanish. Autumn winds mantled our lawn with leaves, but uncovered more questions than answers. My new skin still felt constricting and uncomfortable, but I was grateful to cut myself slack over the unpredictability, relentlessness, and exhaustion of raising children.

Before Thanksgiving, I called my mother to trade stories and gossip. When we paused in the conversation, I took a deep breath.

"I don't know how you did it, Mom. Raising eleven of us. Alone."

"¡Ay, mijita! It was a different time." She was modest.

"No, really. How did you do it?" I could hear her stirring her coffee. "I can barely get through one day sometimes without going crazy."

She laughed.

"I finally get why you threw potatoes at us," I giggled and watched the boys play outside. "I would have, too."

She choked up. "Gracias, mijita."

I credit our sons for giving me the ability to begin forgiving my mother for her mistakes and myself for mine.

EPILOGUE

A few weeks after the Millennium, I railed at Marty one night after a neighborhood party where he'd captivated a large group of folks with our adoption story. I'd squirmed, failed to change the subject, and excused myself halfway through the story. I needed to change Ricardo's training diaper, and we left. I crossed the street to our house relieved to be out of the spotlight. I didn't return to the party.

"I just don't feel heroic! I made a ton of mistakes."

"You did the best you could, Liz. Look at how great the boys are doing." Marty looked me squarely in the eyes and said, "When are you going to stop being so hard on yourself?"

About a year later, I'd told Ms. C, our family therapist, that I had dreamt I was featured on a most wanted poster for being a mother imposter. My poster was featured at the very top of a massive neon billboard, much larger than the ones for murderers and kidnappers and boasted the largest reward in California history.

The therapist nodded, but I couldn't decipher whether she agreed or merely wanted to lure me in. My paranoia shot out tentacles of dread. Was she bound like a priest or lawyer to keep our sessions confidential? When I voiced my concern, she assured me it was her professional obligation.

"I'm still not sure I should've become a mom." I winced. My body collapsed, hands wringing in between my laps, ankles crossed, bracing myself for a judgmental look or reprisal.

Ms. C nodded. Was she tearing up? Or was it me? "We all feel that way."

"Really?"

"Really."

"I don't want to screw them up."

"You won't, Ms. C recounted tidbits of anonymous past clients' regrets designed to dwarf mine.

"With my luck, a decade or two down the road, the boys will appear on *Jerry Springer* and expose me to the world."

She chuckled, "Let's hope they land on *Oprah* instead." We laughed and I settled back into the deep sofa, arms at my sides.

"What would it take for you to forgive yourself?"

I honestly didn't know.

Months later, in the middle of the night, I woke up flailing from a nightmarish collage of horror: gigantic shadows stalking me as I clutched the boys in my arms, but regardless of my grip, they'd be ripped away while screaming out for me. A seeming escape turned out to be a cage surrounded by monstrous faces that tortured us with knives and spears.

Marty held me. "I'm here. It's only a dream."

I held him back then caught my breath and erupted into racking sobs. "It's not. I still feel afraid."

"But you're home."

"Then why don't I feel different from Juárez?" I recounted how terrified I'd been.

"Under the circumstances, I think you were pretty heroic, Liz."

"But I regret it. I've been so afraid of admitting it to you. The boys deserved a better mom."

A silence. I was grateful for the darkness.

"Hey, I wasn't always sure either."

"Really?"

"Yes."

"When?" Was he sparing my feelings?

"Man, there were plenty of times."

"Why didn't we talk about it?"

"Would it have changed anything?"

I cleared the lump in my throat, "I still wonder."

"But we lucked out." He turned on the light and gave me the tissue box.

I shuddered and blew my nose.

I couldn't get myself to say, but I didn't luck out. It didn't look at all like what I had envisioned.

"Babe, write about it. You need to get all this out before it eats you up."

"I did. It's in the journals, but it's dark, Marty."

"Not all of it."

I rolled my eyes. "Enough."

"Just write."

I yawned then Marty followed me into the boys' bedrooms where we watched them sleep as we leaned against the doorway.

The next morning (without any fanfare or announcement), I headed straight to my office for the top bookshelf and gathered the journals. I opened each hardcover to find that month's calendar sketched out and filled with crossed out dates next to a list of phone numbers for doctors, social worker's, DHL, lawyers, María outlined in stars or the boys' latest height, weight, and shoe size. The back covers held book titles, more phone numbers, e-mail addresses, and drawings. I ran my fingers across the scotch tape that held my priceless collection of firsts.

Agustín's handpicked flower petals were carefully assembled next to my proud description of his graceful swimming skills, while Ricardo's delicate leaf adorned the top corner of a page that captured a sweet moment between us earlier that day. The pages were dappled with affirmations that shared space with tiny wads of chewed-up bubblegum taped at the top like Morse code. Some of the entries filled me with such incredible joy that I actually hugged the journal to my chest. I spent hours rereading Ricardo's first phrases, new words, and his beaming reactions to new fruit he was offered. Crayon outlines of their tiny hands next to the scribbles and loops of names. Other pages contained recipes from my neighbors, the words to songs we liked from videos and the ones Agustín made up, notes from Oprah's shows, detailed flow charts of the adoption process, and my dreams.

I had chronicled our entire day—every single day—without fail or fault. I documented the phone calls I made to Marty, my mother-in-law, and friends. I made some acquaintances at the Suites Victoria apartment complex, but my two best friends in Juárez were the public telephones and the Ladatel phone cards. A chunk of chip embedded in a smooth two by three inch thick plastic adorned with exquisite photographs of Mexican destinations, pottery, cinema, and art. I kept them all. They became my lifeline. My worry stone. I clutched expired cards in my palm and rubbed with my thumb as I waited for and received bad news over and over again. They kept time. The stacks on my nightstand towered over my clock, my glass of water. I'd also gone through an amazing number of pens as I bushwhacked my way through the motherhood maze.

Ultimately, I had to make peace with my doubts and regrets for the sake of my sons. There were many things I brought to my mothering plate that I shouldn't have, but there was one thing I knew from the moment we walked out of DIF with our boys in our arms—it was no longer about me. Though Agustín and Ricardo were sweet, loving babies happy to have their own parents, they were undergoing a huge change. They were no longer part of the orphanage, and Agustín missed his playmates and the staff on top of intensely missing his birthparents and waiting to go home. Our oldest was acting out what none of us truly understood at the time. He longed for his old life and family in México.

The disappointment I felt in myself tamped down what I believed should have been a marvelous time for us as new parents. I wish I had been gracious like Audrey Hepburn, navigating through despair and red tape with a serene smile, exuding a sense of calm. I hadn't been.

I reread how we fumbled and favored our way through each day, building a structure that provided the much-needed anchor for our stay in Juárez and ultimately the foundation for our daily routine. I marveled and laughed as I read how the boys wanted to help with every aspect of housecleaning, laundry, and cooking. How long would that last?

My journals testified, when I couldn't, to the suffocating isolation, the boys' strong wills, and worst of all, the gut-wrenching fear I felt in Juárez. It was painful to revisit those foul days when I became a woman, who at times, I didn't even recognize. But I also revisited our nightly prayers, daily meals, and walks to the park that my grandparents and parents had proudly passed on and without skipping a beat, I'd remembered.

Once I'd reread the journals, I knew I'd be able to write the book. And while it was painful to admit to my intense doubts and regrets about becoming a parent at all, I now could see how those feelings had given me the insight and compassion for my oldest son, who more than anything else wanted his first mother to find him. I knew Agustín loved us dearly, but I could understand how he felt about getting us as his parents, specifically me, and not his idealized birthmother. How his door had closed. He was stuck with us.

Agustín said it best while working on a third-grade writing assignment: a condolence letter to a friend of his teacher's who had lost his wife. He wrote in his best pen-manship, "I know how you feel. I had to lose one whole family to get the family I have now."

I let go of the mother I expected myself to be to accept the mother I was meant to be.